fasting

exploring a great spiritual practice

fasting

Carol Garibaldi Rogers

John Kirvan, series editor

SORIN BOOKS Notre Dame, Indiana

www.avemariapress.com

International Standard Book Number: 1-893732-64-9

Cover and text design by Katherine Robinson Coleman

Printed and bound in the United States of America.

Rogers, Carole G.
  Fasting / Carole Garibaldi Rogers.
      p. cm. — (Exploring a great spiritual practice)
  Includes bibliographical references.
  ISBN 1-893732-64-9 (pbk.)
  1. Fasts and feasts. I. Title. II. Series.
BL590.R64 2004
204'.47—dc22
                                                    2004008718

Contents

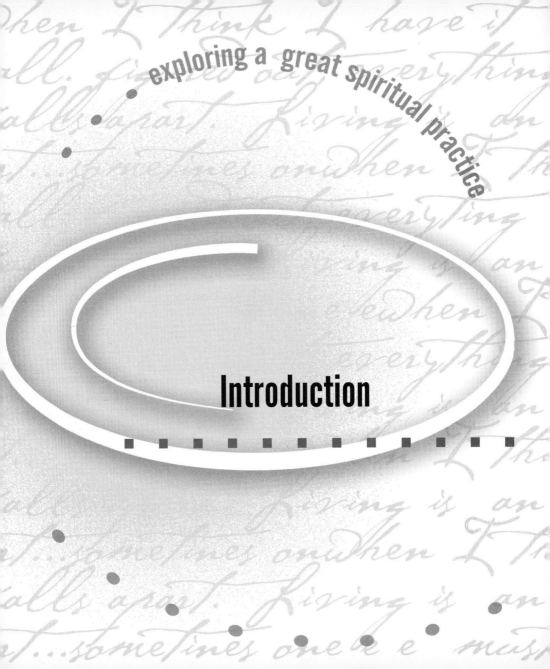

exploring a great spiritual practice

Introduction

We may know that Moses fasted before receiving the Ten Commandments on Mount Sinai. Or that Jesus fasted for forty days in the desert before beginning his public ministry. Or that observant Muslims fast every day during the month of Ramadan. Or that Mahatma Gandhi brought the Hindu tradition of fasting to the world's attention with his rigorous fasts. We may know people who fast as a personal spiritual discipline. But, chances are, we still distance ourselves from the idea of making a personal commitment to fasting. Not us. Not me. Not now.

There are many reasons for reluctance.

♦ Fasting is difficult. To begin is difficult; to continue is also difficult.

♦ Fasting is unpopular. In an era when 54 percent of all Americans are overweight and we can (and do) eat everywhere all the time—in our cars, on the sidewalks, at games, during intermissions, mid-morning, mid-afternoon, and midnight—it is certainly counter-cultural.

♦ Fasting is an experience of limitations. The focus of much contemporary self-help or inspirational literature is on moving beyond barriers, removing restrictions. Our hectic lives impose enough limitations on our freedom. Why would we seek to impose additional limits?

◆ Fasting is confusing. The rules, if there are any, are unclear. What is allowed and what isn't? When is the season for fasting—and how long does it last?

No wonder then that for many of us who seek a deeper spiritual life fasting falls to the bottom of the to-do list. And yet the wisdom of many spiritual traditions tells us that fasting is significant. Thomas Ryan writes: "The person who fasts stands in a noble tradition. In the religious experience of humankind, fasting has always been a prelude and a means to a deeper spiritual life."

Where Does Fasting Come From?

Fasting, according to a simple and frequently used definition, is the partial or complete abstinence from food and drink for a specified length of time. Fasting, thus defined, has been part of almost every religion from ancient pagan practices to Judaism, Christianity, Islam, and Native American rituals.

Historians and anthropologists can provide no single origin for the practice of fasting, which seems to have been a universal experience. It was common in both Eastern and Western cultures and it fulfilled a variety of human needs. In some early religions, fasting was an attempt to gain control over natural elements, allowing one access to a deity or higher power or transcendent being. Fasting often occurred in connection with death and may have been a rite of mourning. Some ancient civilizations viewed fasting as a ritual cleansing, a purification before embarking on a particularly difficult task. These purification fasts might be public, for example that of a king before he began his reign, or private, like a youth entering adulthood and passing through his vision quest.

In biblical Judaism, fasting was one way of "bending the ear of Yahweh," of asking God to grant a favor. The early Christians continued the practice of fasting and viewed it, as Judaism did, as one of the three central disciplines of the spiritual life—prayer, fasting, and almsgiving. Islam, from its earliest history, taught that praise and thanksgiving were essential dimensions of Ramadan fasting. Within these faiths, as well as in secular traditions, fasting also conveyed an ethical imperative: an individual or a community facing a particular trial or dilemma fasted to strengthen character and resolve.

Through the centuries, fasting was thus a sign that expressed deep realities. For some it provided a way to reach

> "The person who **fasts** stands in a **noble** tradition. In the religious experience of **humankind,** fasting has always been a prelude and a means to a **deeper** spiritual life."
>
> *Thomas Ryan*

out to a deity; for others, a way to enhance their human freedom; for still others, a way to connect with nature. Like most human endeavors, the practice has over the years fallen prey to ignorance, extreme interpretations, and confusion. Today's spiritual seekers touch back into the multi-layered history of fasting, seeking the wisdom of the traditions. But they also temper that history with contemporary insights.

How Do We Understand Fasting?

There are as many ways of fasting as there are traditions. Although modern interpretations allow for fasting from other behaviors, the customary meaning of the term has involved the universal human symbols of food and drink. (One of the Hebrew terms for fasting, *sum,* catches this sense. It means, quite literally, "to cover the mouth.") But the term is elastic and within the basic definition there are still more distinctions to be made. Fasting can be described:

◆ By the kind and amount of food and liquid that is allowed. In one type of fasting, practitioners take no food and no liquid, except water. A more restricted version of this fasting allows no water. That is the regimen, for example, of the annual Yom Kippur fast in Judaism. Other fasts restrict the amount or the kind of food that may be eaten, for example, the Lenten fasts among Roman Catholics and Eastern Orthodox Christians. Those who fast for personal reasons will often choose a variation of this partial or limited fast.

◆ By the duration of the fast and its frequency. Most fasts last a day, either from sunup to sunset or for twenty-four hours. Some rigorous fasts last forty days, a period of time that some evangelical Christians recommend because it is rooted in the Bible. A fast may be repetitive—occurring once a week, as some Hindus fast, or every day for a month, as Muslims fast during Ramadan—or occasional, brought on by a religious feast, a dream, or a specific petition to God.

◆ By the surroundings. Some people fast in private, as part of their personal prayer life. At other times, the fast is public, either within a specific congregation or extending worldwide to all members of a particular faith, and the sense of community identification enhances the spiritual dimension of the practice. Those who fast for political reasons are often part of a group and may be participating in a demonstration or march or vigil together.

◆ By motivation. Human motivations are indeed complex. One cannot assume that those who fast for a secular reason are without any religious motive or that religious fasting has nothing to do with secular motivations. Contemporary fasters often combine a variety of seemingly secular motives, some of which actually echo early religious cultures. In prior civilizations, people also fasted to clean their bodies of toxins, to enhance their self-image, or to tap into a source of more energy. They, too, may have wanted to express solidarity with others who were hungry or to strengthen their moral character.

Our concern is primarily with the religious or spiritual motivations for fasting. These can—and often do—exist along with secular purposes, but for spiritual seekers this extra dimension is essential. And it is the spiritual dimension that this book explores.

A Matter of Perspective

This book is meant to be an adventure. We are searching for threads from traditions and contemporary practices that, woven together, may give the discipline of fasting meaning and magnetism. Ours is a spiritual journey.

You will quite rightly want to know about the guide who takes you on this search. I write as a Catholic Christian woman with a Jewish heritage and an ever-deepening respect for eastern religions. These last months, as I have worked on the manuscript, old friends and new acquaintances have asked a common question: "Have you ever fasted?" Yes, I have fasted and I have experienced the deep spiritual resonance that fasting can bring to prayer and meditation. But this book is not about my experiences. My task was to read a great many books and articles, interview a host of people, and distill for you what I have learned. My own understanding of fasting has been significantly enriched and expanded by my research and my conversations. I hope you will have a similar response.

Using This Book

In an age when the word itself is ambiguous, the traditions remote, and the culture unfriendly, we are attempting to answer the basic question: Why fast? You will want to use this book in ways that best suit you. But here's what you'll find in each section.

◆ In Part I, we will search for the wisdom of the traditions, first looking at the practice as it comes to us from the three monotheistic religions of Judaism, Christianity, and Islam, and then broadening our perspective to include other religions in which fasting has been important. We will focus on the core of the traditions, as I perceive them, and not linger on the extreme, albeit pious, asceticism that is present in all religions.

◆ In Part II, we will look first at contemporary practices of fasting during the seasons or times specifically prescribed by religious traditions—Yom Kippur, Lent, and Ramadan. How do individual Americans observe these times of fasting? We will then explore some of the other reasons contemporary people fast—for personal, political, and holistic motivations. Accompanying each of these six chapters are "Voices"—first-person accounts by real people who fast in one of the ways the chapter describes.

◆   In a final chapter, we will try to find a perspective from which to evaluate what we have learned.

By the end of this journey together, I hope I will have provided enough information to answer two questions: Is there a place for fasting in present-day spirituality? How could such a discipline be constructed in light of the wisdom of the traditions but also informed by contemporary insights and concerns? If there are satisfactory answers to those questions, some of us will perhaps reclaim a tradition and reinvigorate a spiritual discipline, incorporating it into our busy contemporary lives—for our own betterment and that of the world around us.

Wisdom
fromthe Traditions

Fasting is an invitation to still the noise and listen to the silence, to cut the clutter and see the order, and to slide beneath what is superficial and trivial to that which is worthwhile and lasting.

David Trembley

exploring a great spiritual practice

chapterone

Judaism

Biblical Jews believed in a very personal God, a God who had made a covenant with them, who would stand by them in times of distress, who would listen to their prayers and petitions, and to whom they, in turn, were to remain faithful. The earliest Jewish stories of God's relationship with humanity are recorded in the Hebrew Scriptures, which the Jews also call *Tanakh* and Christians sometimes call the Old Testament. It is here that we will begin.

Because contemporary Jews do not live by Scripture alone, but by the teachings of generations of rabbis, we will continue with a look at fasting in the Talmud, the written collection of early rabbinic law and interpretation. We will conclude this chapter with a brief look at what contributions to our understanding of fasting can come from Kabbalah, the Jewish mystical tradition.

Judaism, both in the Scriptures and in the Talmud, teaches wisely on the subject of fasting. Christianity and Islam, both of which developed from Judaism, offer additional richness.

The Hebrew Scriptures

T he origin of fasting among the Jewish people is obscure, but the Bible records many instances of both individual and community fasts. Moses, David, Elijah, and Daniel fasted; so did Ezra, Esther, and Nehemiah. It is clear from several references (Jonah 3:7 and Ezra 10:6, for example) that the Jews understood fasting to mean abstaining from all food and drink for a period of time—be it for three days, from sundown of one day to sundown of the next, or from sunup to sundown of the same day. But, as the rabbis later explained, fasting was also to be considered as part of a larger effort of self-denial, as a way of humbling oneself before God.

Biblical Jews fasted for a number of reasons, but whatever the reason, there was an underlying spiritual dimension to the practice. By looking at a few specific passages, we can begin to appreciate how fasting expressed their understanding of their relationship with God.

◆ Fasting on the Day of Atonement (Yom Kippur) is the most important and the most serious of the biblical fasts. Mandated by the Mosaic Law, set down in the Scriptures in both Leviticus and Numbers, and interpreted in the teachings of the ancient rabbis, this community-wide fast is still observed by all branches of Judaism.

◆ God tells Moses: "And this shall be to you a law for all time: In the seventh month, on the tenth day of the month, you shall practice self-denial: and you shall do no manner of work, neither the citizen nor the alien who resides among you. For on this day atonement shall be made for you to cleanse you of all your sins; you shall be clean before the Lord. It shall be a Sabbath of complete rest for you, and you shall practice self-denial; it is a law for all time." (Leviticus 16:29–31).

◆ The purpose of the fast is clear from the words in the passage; the people were to make atonement for their sins, to cleanse themselves of past offenses before beginning another year.

◆ As Moses was leading the Jewish people out of Egypt to "the land of milk and honey," the Lord asks him to carve two stone tablets and come to the top of Mt. Sinai. Exodus records: "And he was there with the Lord forty days and forty nights; he ate no bread and drank no water; and he wrote down on the tablets the terms of the covenant, the Ten

Commandments" (34:28). Exodus doesn't explain why Moses fasted on Mt. Sinai, but subsequent teachings suggest that he may have been atoning for the sins of his people who had been "defiant toward the Lord" as they wandered in the desert for forty years. As their leader, he sought God's compassion on them.

This sense becomes clearer with a passage from Deuteronomy. When Moses came down from Mt. Sinai, he found the people had again strayed from the path of the Lord. We read: "I threw myself down before the Lord—eating no bread and drinking no wine forty days and forty nights as before—because of the great wrong you had committed, doing what displeased the Lord and vexing Him. For I was in dread of the Lord's fierce anger against you . . . "(9:18–19).

One cannot live by bread alone, but by every word that comes from the mouth of God.

Moses' fast, alone on the mountain, can also be seen as an eloquent expression of human limitations while encountering the power of God. When Jesus, fasting in the desert for forty days, is tempted by the devil, he replies, "One cannot live by bread alone, but by every word that comes from the mouth of God." That, in turn, is a quotation from Deuteronomy 8:3, recalling the words of Moses to the people in the desert.

◆ God sends the prophet Elijah to convey bad news to King Ahab of Israel. Because Ahab had committed himself to evil, the Lord would bring disaster upon him. The Hebrew Scriptures say: "When Ahab heard these words he rent his clothes and put sackcloth on his body. He fasted and lay in sackcloth and walked about subdued" (1Kings 21:27). The Lord then tells Elijah that he has seen "how Ahab humbled himself before Me" and he will not bring disaster to Ahab in his lifetime.

In this individual fast, dramatically described, Ahab seeks God's compassion and averts a tragedy. Here, and in many other examples from the Hebrew Scriptures, we see evidence that the Jewish people believed fasting was a way to "bend the ear of Yahweh," to express their remorse, either individually or as a community, for actions that offended their God.

◆ At other times the Jews fasted to avert a calamity that was not the result of their sins. When Queen Esther is warned that the king intends to slaughter all the Jews in the kingdom, she, all her handmaids, and all the Jews in the kingdom fast for three days before she approaches the king to plead for the Jews. Queen Esther faced death if she approached the king without being called, but the king learns the truth behind the plot and spares the Jews. The book of Esther records: "In every province and in every city when the king's command and decree arrived, there was gladness and joy among the Jews, a feast and a holiday" (8:17).

Jews in biblical times lived a precarious existence. They faced both military hostilities and natural dangers; wars, persecution, and drought were common occurrences. Fasting was often a spontaneous way to seek God's protection when peril seemed imminent or when a task seemed overwhelming. They prayed and fasted with confidence that their God, with whom they had an enduring personal relationship, would respond.

Some of the biblical Jews, like some Christians in later eras, erred in the way they fasted. In their zeal to punish the body, these Jews ignored an essential teaching of Judaism: that all life, including our human bodies, comes from God, and all that comes from God is good. Other Jews made the exterior actions of fasting and self-denial of primary importance, forgetting the inner motivation, the turning toward God that had also been an indispensable mark of fasting in the Hebrew Scriptures.

It became the role of the prophets to call attention to the empty charade of fasting that is not accompanied by a change of heart.

◆ Joel reminds the people of their obligations, but also of the goodness of their God: "Yet even now—says the Lord—turn back to me with all your hearts, with fasting, weeping, and lamenting; rend your hearts rather than your garments, and turn back to the Lord your God. For he is gracious and compassionate, slow to anger, abounding in kindness, and renouncing punishment"

(2:12–13). For Joel, personal religious authenticity is essential.

◆ Isaiah presents a dialogue between the people and God. The people ask: "Why, when we fasted, did You not see? When we starved our bodies, did You pay no heed?" And God replies: "Because on your fast day you see to business and oppress all your laborers! Because you fast in strife and contention, and you strike with a wicked fist! Your fasting today is not such as to make your voice heard on high. Is such the fast I desire, a day for men to starve their bodies? . . . Do you call that a fast, a day when the Lord is favorable? No, this is the fast I desire: to unlock fetters of wickedness, and untie the cords of the yoke, to let the oppressed go free; to break off every yoke. It is to share your bread with the hungry, and to take the wretched poor into your home; when you see the naked, to clothe him, and not to ignore your own kin" (58:3–7).

Isaiah decried self-centered denial and linked proper fasting with concern for justice and care for the poor. Later Jewish rabbis and scholars would discuss what Isaiah really meant. Was he suggesting an end to all fasting? That is unlikely, they concluded. Both Joel and Isaiah saw that the practice of fasting needed a corrective. They were telling the

Reading the **Talmud** is an encounter with **human beings, wise** human beings, as they struggle to **understand God,** each other, and all the complex relationships that result.

people that the external physical action of fasting, if it is not accompanied by justice and love, is empty. It is interior repentance or change of heart that God desires. That is the true fast that leads to God's forgiveness.

This passage from Isaiah is essential to understanding the Jewish concept of fasting. It is read every year during the morning service on Yom Kippur. (See chapter 7.)

Rabbinic Teachings

The teachings of the ancient rabbis are found in the Talmud, which remains the core of Jewish teaching and practice. Reading the Talmud is an encounter with human beings, wise human beings, as they struggle to understand God, each other, and all the complex relationships that result. Contemporary rabbis warn that one does not read the Talmud; one studies it—usually for a lifetime. Then perhaps its wisdom becomes evident. We must make do with a shorter exploration, because in the Talmud we find some fundamental insights into the Jewish tradition of fasting.

◆ The most important fast of the Jewish calendar is Yom Kippur, and the rabbis devote an entire *tractate* (or chapter) to clarify what fasting on that day means. We can read: "On the Day of Atonement it is forbidden to eat or drink, or bathe or anoint oneself or put on sandals or to indulge in conjugal intercourse." Despite the significance of the fast, however, the rabbis are moderate, allowing exceptions and dispensations—for those who were ill, for pregnant women, for children.

◆ The Talmud confirms four additional communal fast days first named in Scripture by Nehemiah. These four dates commemorate historical tragedies, such as the fall of Jerusalem or the destruction of the temple. The rabbis define the length of the fasts: on Yom Kippur and on Tisha b'Av, a holy day that falls in the summer months, the fast shall last from sunset to sunset of the following day. All other fast days are from sunrise until sunset of the same day. (Contemporary Reform Judaism recognizes only Yom Kippur as a fast day. Orthodox Jews and some Conservative Jews also observe Tisha b'Av. Only Orthodox Jews observe the other three commemorative fast days and for many of them it is now a struggle to find contemporary relevance in these observances.)

◆ The Jewish commitment to the Sabbath is clear; the rabbis rule that with the exception of Yom Kippur, any fast day that falls on a Sabbath must be postponed.

◆ Fasting in Jewish tradition is primarily communal. For times of drought, the Talmud prescribed a carefully calibrated community fast, gradually increasing the length of the fast and expanding the number of individuals involved until the rains came. But the rabbis did also allow occasional private fasts, to avert the consequences of a bad dream, for example, or to mark the anniversary of the death of a parent or teacher. Brides and grooms fasted on their wedding day before the ceremony.

◆ The rabbis were opposed to severe ascetic practices. They repeatedly asserted the Jewish belief that all of God's creation is good, including our bodies. One Talmudic proverb cautions, "A man is to give account in the hereafter for any permissible pleasure from which he abstained." And another rabbi ruled: "A private individual must not fast excessively, lest he become a burden on the public, and the public should be forced to support him."

Our brief look at the Hebrew Scriptures and the Talmud indicates that fasting has played in important role in Judaism. The wisdom from the tradition clearly says fasting must not be an end in itself—a self-indulgent asceticism that turns inward. For the Jews, fasting should be a way of connecting with God and with others.

Wisdom from Kabbalah

Often described as Jewish mysticism, Kabbalah has been misunderstood, derided, and marginalized for centuries. Rabbis traditionally taught that one could not approach Kabbalah until one was well educated in the Torah and the Talmud. And yet Kabbalah, which became a recognized movement in the Middle Ages, has retained its appeal for many people (not all of them Jewish) who seek a deeper spiritual connection to God.

At its essence, Kabbalah is not magic or divination or an easy way to find serenity in troubled times. It is a way of studying the hidden life of God. And it is a serious attempt to build an awareness of the presence of God in our lives while still acknowledging God's transcendence. In this understanding, it has some shared characteristics with other mystical traditions.

One contemporary rabbi who has carefully studied Kabbalah and mined its meaning in contexts that add to our discussion of fasting is Rabbi Nilton Bonder, who is known as "the Green Rabbi" for his work in social and environmental causes. Bonder has written a trilogy that includes *The Kabbalah of Food*. There, he has searched the Jewish tradition for holistic wisdom about food on "physical, emotional, social, and spiritual planes."

Using Kabbalah's four worlds or dimensions of reality, Bonder situates fasting in the spiritual dimension, the source of Divine energy. Fasting in this world, he says, does not mean to abstain from eating, but "to actively feed oneself with nothing." Fasting "represents the perfect merging of our physical and spiritual natures."

Bonder's book makes some other important points.

◆ "God resides in a person who is a whole being." Fasting is not a break with creation; it is not "an act of neglect." Fasting must be an act that strengthens our harmony with creation.

◆ Fasting "allows for the recognition of a special kind of hunger that can only be satisfied by not eating. This discovery provides us with a new vision of life that is profoundly healing."

◆ When we fast "as a way of making a return to life out of our awareness of its bounty toward us—we reach a special level in the art of giving and receiving." We are expressing our consciousness of the wider universe in which we exist.

◆ Fasting can bring us insights into ecology and a way of assessing our concern for the environment versus our habits of consumption.

Fasting must be an act that strengthens our harmony with creation.

A Word about Time

Judaism is a religion that reverences time. The Bible tells the story of God in human history, and Jewish faith draws many of its important themes from the dimension of time—biblical past, our present, and messianic future. The Jews, wherever they find themselves, have continued to honor the memory of sacred events. Judaism regards the Sabbath as a break in ordinary time, the reverent focus of each week; and its holy days move with the lunar calendar, in rhythm with the seasons. The Jewish sense of fasting is embedded in this sense of holy time. Fasting can connect us with the cycles of our own days, seasons, and years.

"The higher goal of spiritual living," Rabbi Abraham Joshua Heschel writes, "is not to amass a wealth of information, but to face sacred moments. . . . A moment of insight is a fortune, transporting us beyond the confines of measured time." Our search for insights about fasting can benefit from the Jewish sense of time and from Rabbi Heschel's wisdom.

"The higher goal of **spiritual** living is not to amass a wealth of information, but to face **sacred moments. . . .** A moment of **insight** is a fortune, transporting us **beyond** the confines of **measured time.**"

Rabbi Abraham Joshua Heschel

exploring a great spiritual practice

chaptertwo

Christianity
Jesus and
the Gospels

The Jews of the biblical era understood their complete dependence on God; fasting was one way of expressing their awareness of that relationship. This idea, so clearly linked with interior motivation and the true meaning of humility, is also significant in Christian teaching on fasting.

When we search for the wisdom of fasting in Christianity we tap into two sources: Scripture, which comprises both the Hebrew Scriptures (or Old Testament) and the Christian Scriptures (or New Testament), and tradition, which consists of later developments in Christianity. Our search begins in the New Testament, with the Gospel narratives, which relate the life of Jesus Christ, whom Christians believe is the Messiah, the promised Son of God, and who taught by both his example and his words. This chapter looks closely at four relevant Gospel passages. The two following chapters will trace the discipline of Christian fasting as it evolved through the centuries.

The Fast in the Desert

Jesus was an observant and knowledgeable Jew; he lived in a Jewish world. He prayed as a Jew and worshipped as a Jew. We are presented with early reminders of that heritage when we read the accounts of Jesus fasting for forty days in the desert. Like Moses and other Hebrew prophets, Jesus retreated to the wilderness to meet his God. The period of time he fasted—forty days—is reminiscent of the forty years the Jews wandered in the desert. After each temptation, Jesus responds to the devil with words from the book of Deuteronomy—words that Jesus as a good Jew would have known well.

The time Jesus spent fasting in the desert is described in the gospels of Matthew, Mark, and Luke; each gospel writer places the event after the baptism of Jesus by John the Baptist, during which Jesus is proclaimed the Son of God. The way

Jesus acts while he is in the desert thus becomes both a reflection of the kind of messiah he is and a model for the way his followers should behave. The gospels show Jesus as a messiah interested in spiritual matters, in justice, and in a right relationship with God; not in bread, wealth, and power. Christians must cultivate a similar lifestyle—one that reflects their commitment to matters beyond temporal desires.

In this early gospel narrative, even before Jesus begins his public ministry, Jesus' actions display the characteristics of a proper relationship with God. Here are the words from the Gospel of Matthew:

Then Jesus was led up by the Spirit into the wilderness to be tempted by the devil. He fasted forty days and forty nights, and afterwards he was famished. The tempter came and said to him, "If you are the Son of God, command these stones to become loaves of bread." But he answered, "It is written, 'One does not live by bread alone, but by every word that comes from the mouth of God.'"

Then the devil took him to the holy city and placed him on the pinnacle of the

temple, saying to him, "If you are the Son of God, throw yourself down; for it is written, 'He will command his angels concerning you,' and 'On their hands they will bear you up, so that you will not dash your foot against a stone.'" Jesus said to him, "Again it is written, 'Do not put the Lord your God to the test.'"

Again, the devil took him to a very high mountain and showed him all the kingdoms of the world and their splendor and he said to him, "All these I will give you, if you will fall down and worship me." Jesus said to him, "Away with you, Satan! For it is written, 'Worship the Lord your God, and serve only him.'"

Then the devil left him and suddenly angels came and waited on him. (4:1–11)

What does this story convey about the way Jesus experienced fasting? And what does it say about the reasons Christians fast? There are several important clues in the narrative:

◆ Jesus is led by the Spirit into the desert. The gospel writers are saying that Jesus did not act from his own agenda; God prompted this retreat and Jesus responded.

◆ Jesus is hungry after his fast—a clearly human reaction. The length of time for the fast is not as important as the actions. Jesus is hungry and yet he is able to withstand the temptations and remain faithful to God.

◆ Each of the temptations reaches a different level of human weakness—a desire for material objects like food, a desire for status or wealth, a desire for authority over others. When Jesus refuses the invitation of the first temptation—to change stones into bread—he is placing food in its proper context. Human beings must find meaning in a higher source of nourishment—the word of God. In resisting the second temptation, Jesus asserts the right relationship of a Son to the Father; one does not taunt the other. The same attitude of humility should govern the relationship of his followers to their God and to one another. In withstanding the final temptation, Jesus asserts that worship belongs only to God. For Christians, that can mean confronting the many idols that occur in their lifetimes. It can also mean fostering a deep concern for all God's creatures, for those who are weak, threatened, and without protection.

Human beings must find meaning in a higher source of nourishment—the word of God.

◆ Jesus leaves the desert and begins his ministry. Pushing the discipline of fasting too far leaves us rigid and self-centered, far from others instead of in solidarity with them. Jesus did not remain in the wilderness, living a private ascetic life, but went out among the people, healing, comforting, befriending. The Christian message is that fasting strengthens us for love.

For Christians, this episode can be a lesson in setting proper priorities. Joseph Wimmer writes, "In the midst of the hunger, fear, and deprivation of fasting, a new horizon appears. We become aware that things of the spirit are superior, that we must not limit our concerns only to the cares of this world, to the accumulation and enjoyment of temporal goods. We gradually realize what it means to live by every word that comes from the mouth of God."

In the Scriptures, the "greatest and first commandment" urges people to love God with all their hearts, with all their souls, with all their minds. It is possible, Christians say, to read the entire description of Jesus' fast in the desert as a meditation on such love of God.

Teaching on Prayer, Fasting, and Almsgiving

The Gospel of Matthew also contains another key text on fasting. Here Matthew presents the words of Jesus instead of describing his actions. Found in the middle of the lengthy Sermon on the Mount, in which Jesus teaches his disciples the Beatitudes and many other essentials of the Christian life, this passage has been the primary source of Christian teaching on the spiritual disciplines of prayer, fasting, and almsgiving from the second century into the present.

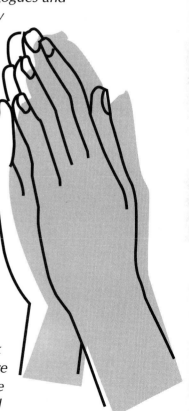

So whenever you give alms, do not sound a trumpet before you, as the hypocrites do in the synagogues and in the streets, so that they may be praised by others. Truly I tell you, they have received their reward. But when you give alms, do not let your left hand know what your right hand is doing, so that your alms may be done in secret; and your Father who sees in secret will reward you.

And whenever you pray, do not be like the hypocrites; for they love to stand and pray in the synagogues and at the street corners, so that they may be seen by others. Truly I tell you, they have received their reward. But whenever you pray, go into your room and shut the door and pray to your Father who is in secret; and your Father who sees in secret will reward you. . . .

And whenever you fast, do not look dismal, like the hypocrites, for they disfigure their faces so as to show others that they are fasting. Truly I tell you, they have received their reward. But when you fast, put oil on your head and wash your face, so that your fasting may be seen not by others but by your Father who is in secret; and your Father who sees in secret will reward you. (Mt 6:2–18)

This passage, which groups the three spiritual disciplines in balanced, almost rhythmical verses, is original with Matthew. The literary genre, biblical scholars say, is catechesis. And hearing the simple repetitions, reminiscent of childhood rhymes, it is easy to understand how these verses could instruct people who did not read.

They can also instruct contemporary spiritual seekers.

◆ The teaching on each practice follows a pleasing pattern. All three have an identical structure, enhanced by vivid descriptive language. We are lured into attention.

◆ Each passage begins with the word "when." Notice that Jesus does not use "if." He assumes that these important disciplines are a part of his listeners' lives—those who were present at the Sermon on the Mount, those in early Christian times who first heard the gospels proclaimed, and contemporary listeners.

◆ Fasting is as important in the teaching of Jesus as prayer and almsgiving. All three are similarly recommended. Each practice receives an equal number of verses (two) and each begins with a negative description of the practice (what not to do) and moves on to a recommended pattern of behavior (what to do).

These eight verses have been a rich source for Christian teaching through the ages and lie close to the heart of essential Christian truths. The disciplines of prayer, fasting, and almsgiving encourage Christians to turn their attention away from themselves and toward God and others. The three practices are intimately linked in this passage and should be similarly linked in Christian lives.

The disciplines of prayer, fasting, and almsgiving encourage Christians to turn their attention away from themselves and toward God and others.

Parable of the Pharisee and the Tax Collector

Jesus often told parables to bring his message alive. In the parable of the Pharisee and the tax collector, unique to the Gospel of Luke, Jesus is teaching about proper motivation for spiritual practices, about the need for interior honesty, humility, and integrity.

He also told this parable to some who trusted in themselves that they were righteous and regarded others with contempt. "Two men went up to the temple to pray, one a Pharisee and the other a tax collector. The Pharisee, standing by himself, was praying thus, 'God, I thank you that I am not like other people: thieves, rogues, adulterers, or even like this tax collector. I fast twice a week; I give a tenth of all my income.' But the tax collector, standing far off, would not even look up to heaven, but was beating his breast and saying, 'God, be merciful to me, a sinner!' I tell you, this man went down to his home justified rather than the other; for all who exalt themselves will be humbled, but all who humble themselves will be exalted." (Luke 18: 9–14).

The parable provides clear evidence that many Jews of Jesus' time did indeed follow the three practices of prayer, fasting, and almsgiving. But it's also obvious from the parable that not all of them understood the proper motivation for the practices.

A close reading of the parable reveals what a proper attitude might be.

◆ The two characters, drawn with minimal descriptions, are useful narrative tools—stereotypes of the sinful person and the good person.

◆ The boastful prayer of the Pharisee who tells God how he tithes and fasts twice a week is obviously offensive. Does it need any further elaboration? Yet Jesus strengthens his message by providing not only a comparison with the prayer and behavior of the tax collector but also a clear rebuke.

◆ Humility before God is an essential element in fasting. Those who hear the lesson of the parable cannot allow themselves to feel superior to others who do not fast.

The Jesus Prayer: "Lord Jesus Christ, Son of the living God, have mercy on me, a sinner."

The words of the tax collector have held their appeal down through the centuries. They are one of the sources for an ancient but still popular prayer, called simply "The Jesus Prayer": "Lord Jesus Christ, Son of the living God, have mercy on me, a sinner."

Jesus as Bridegroom

In another passage, which appears with similar wording in the gospels of Matthew, Mark, and Luke, Jesus is asked why his disciples don't fast like the Pharisees and those who follow John the Baptist. The answer Jesus gives has often puzzled Christians.

"The days will come when the bridegroom is taken away from them, and then they will fast on that day."

Mark 2:20

Now John's disciples and the Pharisees were fasting; and people came and said to him, "Why do John's disciples and the disciples of the Pharisees fast, but your disciples do not fast?" Jesus said to them, "The wedding guests cannot fast while the bridegroom is with them, can they? As long as they have the bridegroom with them, they cannot fast. The days will come when the bridegroom is taken away from them, and then they will fast on that day." (Mark 2:18–20)

It might seem as if Jesus is dismissing the value of fasting. But biblical scholars say that is unlikely, given his own fast in the desert and his other teachings. They draw a different sense from the passage.

◆ In Scripture, wedding imagery often describes God's intimate relationship with humanity. Jesus is referring to himself as the bridegroom; he is telling his listeners that God is indeed among them.

◆ It has become an enduring image: Jesus as bridegroom— a symbol of joy and happiness and fulfillment. The proper mood for a wedding—for the coming of God into the world—is joy. At a wedding, the guests feast; they do not fast.

◆ Jesus also frees his disciples from the rigid kinds of fasts practiced by John the Baptist and the Pharisees. He frees them—not to lead lives of indulgence, but to celebrate his presence, to enjoy each other's company, and share their meals with the poor and the outcast. The gospels recount many of these occasions.

◆ There are times to feast and times to fast. When Jesus says, "the bridegroom will be taken away from them," he is referring to his own death. His disciples will fast "on that day." The early Christians chose Friday, the day Jesus died, as one of their weekly fast days and scholars suggest that the practice is probably rooted in this gospel verse.

◆ In this conversation, Jesus has not eliminated fasting as a spiritual discipline for his followers. He has placed it in context.

Fasting is not, in Christian understanding, about self-inflicted punishment. It is about imitating Christ, seeking freedom from wrong priorities, finding a way to make God the center of one's life. In the gospels, Jesus gave his followers an attitude, a focus, and a context for their fasting.

exploring a great spiritual practice

chapter**three**

Christianity
The First
Thousand Years

The Acts of the Apostles, which is a continuation of Luke's gospel, contains firsthand information about the life of the early church after Jesus had left his followers.

As we search for the early Christian understanding of fasting, we find here several important threads. From Acts we learn that the disciples fasted and that the practice was connected in their minds with the prompting of the Holy Spirit and with ministry.

"For three days he was without sight, and neither ate nor drank."

Acts 9:9

♦ Saul, an educated Jew from Tarsus, was one of the fiercest opponents of the early Christians. After a conversion experience on the road to Damascus, he is led by his companions into the city. "For three days he was without sight, and neither ate nor drank." (Acts 9:9) Ananias, a Christian, arrives and lays his hands on Saul. Saul's sight is restored, he is baptized and takes some food. Luke's text places a three-day fast between two encounters with the Holy Spirit, between a call to conversion and baptism.

♦ As the early church grew, the disciples responded to the needs of their new ministry. The disciples are "worshiping the Lord and fasting" when the Holy Spirit asks them to select Barnabas and Saul for "the work to which I have called them." (Acts 13:2). In the following verse, "after fasting and praying" the disciples send the two off to their ministry in other cities. Luke's text demonstrates that prayer and fasting were linked in the lives of the early church.

♦ A similar episode occurs when Saul (subsequently known to Christians as Paul) and Barnabas appointed elders for the churches they visited, "with prayer and fasting they entrusted them to the Lord" (Acts 14:23).

In Acts, there is, however, no description of seasonal or community-wide fasts or any mention of the example Jesus gave in the desert, or of the proper inner disposition for fasting that Jesus taught. These threads began to appear in the following centuries.

The First Centuries

In the first and second generations after the Apostles, there is some evidence of fasting and an effort to preach about it, but the practice was not widely regulated and varied greatly from place to place.

By the end of the first century or the beginning of the second, Wednesdays and Fridays had become days of fasting for Christians. Pious Jews fasted on Mondays and Thursdays, days connected with Moses' ascent and descent from Mount Sinai. Christians selected days that had religious significance for them. Friday commemorated the day Jesus died and Wednesday the day he was betrayed and arrested. For Christians these were not twenty-four-hour fasts or even sunup to sundown fasts; fasting ended with the evening meal, which could be eaten as early as the ninth hour, or 3 PM.

The *Didache*, an early non-Scriptural text also known as *The Teaching of the Twelve Apostles,* recommended a two-day fast prior to baptism. The person to be baptized, the baptizer, and "any others who may be able" were all encouraged to participate.

Early Christians did yet not practice Lenten fasting, as later Christians would, but a short Paschal fast developed in the second century.

Christians were required to fast strictly—total abstinence from any food—for the two days prior to Easter, which became known as Good Friday and Holy Saturday. This pre-Paschal fast lengthened in some places to four or six days, moving backward into the first days of Holy Week. The purpose of the fast was clearly conveyed: Christians were to prepare themselves for the celebration of Jesus' Resurrection.

Because Easter was the time for baptism in the early church, the Paschal fast may also have been a way for the entire community to join the new Christians in their pre-baptism fasting.

The forty-day Lenten fast, as modern Christians know it, had probably evolved by the fourth century. By the end of the fifth century, Lenten fasting had not only become more regulated; it had absorbed a variety of motivations. As in the earlier centuries, Christians fasted in preparation for Easter, as an expression of mourning for "the bridegroom" who had gone, in penitence for sins. They may have understood fasting as imitative of Jesus' forty-day fast in the desert. Fasting had also become an expression of corporate character. It defined the Christian's identity.

There were other seasonal times for fasting in these early years of Christianity. Beginning in the third century, three days in each of the four seasons, known as Ember Days, were set aside for prayer and penitence, which included fasting. During the spring, four days of prayers and processions, called Rogation Days, also gradually became days of fasting. Beginning in the fourth century, a eucharistic fast, which meant no food or drink before receiving communion, became universal.

The early Christians took seriously the idea that fasting accompanied prayer. Fasting was also clearly linked in their minds—and in practice—to almsgiving. Without acts of charity, fasting was not worthwhile.

◆ In *The Shepherd of Hermas*, a collection of visions and ethical precepts written by an unknown author around the year 150, there are several references that connect fasting with giving to the poor. For example:

> *In the day on which you fast you will taste nothing but bread and water; and having reckoned up the price of the dishes of that day which you intended to have eaten, you will give it to a widow, or an orphan, or to some person in want and thus you will exhibit humility*

of mind, so that the one who has received benefit from your humility may fill his own soul.

◆ Origen, a theologian of the second and third centuries, praised all those who fasted "in order to nourish the poor."

◆ Leo the Great, Pope from 440 to 461, preached many sermons on fasting. To give just one example:

> *We order you this fast of December...Let each one rejoice in the copiousness of the harvest...but in such a way that even the poor rejoice in its abundance...Let all make account of their riches and those who have more give more. Let the abstinence of the faithful become the nourishment of the poor and let the indigent receive that which others give up.*

"Do you wish your **prayer** to **fly** toward **God?** Give it two wings: **fasting** and **almsgiving."**

Augustine

◆ Augustine, bishop of Hippo in North Africa from 395 to his death in 430, influential theologian, author of *Confessions*, and powerful preacher, summed it up when he eloquently wrote: "Do you wish your prayer to fly toward God? Give it two wings: fasting and almsgiving."

Did the ordinary Christian in these centuries observe all these fast days? The practice varied from place to place. But Christians probably did observe a kind of fasting on the required occasions. Fasting meant one full meal a day, eaten in the evening or late afternoon. In the early years, the meal was probably only bread and water. Gradually, and in different places, fruit, eggs, fish, and even poultry were added. The discipline of fasting, for most early Christians, with the exception of penitents who were fasting for the forgiveness of their sins, gradually blurred with abstinence from meat. Succeeding centuries saw an increasing trend toward legalism and the regulation of quantities and kinds of food.

Early Monasticism

The faith of Christians during these early years was simple and, as the threat of persecution waned and Christianity was recognized by the Roman government, it was also safe. Some seekers of true holiness believed they needed to break their ties with that world in order to claim salvation. These early monks, who moved to remote desert areas of Egypt and Syria and charted their own paths, were the first Christian hermits.

In solitude, they prayed and fasted. Some of their practices were indeed extreme. Anthony, an Egyptian hermit who was already a Christian hero by the year 400, slept on

These early **monks,** who moved to remote desert areas of **Egypt** and **Syria** and charted their own paths, were the first Christian **hermits.**

the ground, ate only once a day, and drank only water.

Simeon Stylites, from northern Syria, is the first of the oft-sited pillar saints. A monk and then a hermit, he lived on top of a succession of high pillars from 423 to his death in 459. He frequently ate nothing during the forty days of Lent. His extraordinary public prayer, fasting, and penance brought him admiration and influence during his lifetime and canonization after his death.

For other early monks, fasting, observed alone or in community, was a rigorous but far less ostentatious part of their everyday lives. And from them spiritual seekers can hear some wise instructions about the practice of fasting.

Much of this wisdom comes down to us in a small book called *The Wisdom of the Desert* (*Verba Seniorum*), well translated by Thomas Merton. The book is a collection of simple, wonderfully human tales showing the ways an abbot or revered monk taught the novices who gathered around him for instruction in living a holy life. As Merton explains in his introduction to the book, the seekers asked the elder monk for "a word (*verbum*)" that would help them find salvation. Repeatedly, we see that charity and hospitality are more important than "fasting and personal ascetic routines."

Merton writes: "All through the *Verba Seniorum* we find a repeated insistence on the primacy of love over everything else in the spiritual life . . . asceticism, contemplation, solitude, prayer. Love in fact *is* the spiritual life and without it all the other exercises of the spirit, however lofty, are emptied of content."

He concludes that while we cannot do exactly what they did, "we need to learn from these men of the fourth century how to ignore prejudice, defy compulsion and strike out fearlessly into the unknown."

Two brief excerpts from *The Wisdom of the Desert* connect fasting with these lessons that Merton draws from fourth-century hermits.

◆ "A brother asked one of the elders, saying: 'There are two brothers, of whom one remains praying in his cell, fasting six days at a time and doing a great deal of penance. The other one takes care of the sick. Which one's work is more pleasing to God?' The elder replied: 'If that brother who fasts six days at a time were to hang himself up by the nose, he could not equal the one who takes care of the sick.'"

◆ "Once two brethren came to a certain elder whose custom it was not to eat every day. But when he saw the brethren he invited them with joy to dine with him, saying: 'Fasting has its reward, but he who eats out of charity fulfills two commandments, for he sets aside his own will and he refreshes his hungry brethren.'"

Benedict

"Fasting has its reward, but he who eats out of charity fulfills two commandments, for he sets aside his own will and he refreshes his hungry brethren."

Benedict of Nursia, a fifth century Italian monk, is known as the founder of Western monasticism not only because he started communities of monks but also because his *Rule,* a code of behavior that is both spiritual and practical, became the foundation of all Western monastic life. Christians living outside monastery walls have always adopted some variation of monastic ways as their path to holiness and Benedict's *Rule* has remained a significant spiritual guide for Christians through the centuries.

Benedict lived in a time of stern asceticism and political turmoil, but he remained kind and generous and always aware of human weakness. Benedict's ideas about food and drink and moderation surface in several places in his *Rule*. He is reluctant to prescribe specific amounts or kinds of food and drink for individuals who have different needs, strengths, and weaknesses.

While the examples are specific to medieval monasticism, the lessons can be brought into contemporary life. Sister Joan Chittister, a Benedictine nun, does an excellent job of making Benedict's message on fasting accessible.

The *Rule* says, "For nothing is so inconsistent with the life of any Christian as overindulgence." Chittister writes: "Too much of anything, we have discovered, can weigh us down. Each of us needs to fast from something to bring ourselves to the summit of our spiritual powers. The question is whether or not we have lost a sense of the value of fasting or do we simply fill ourselves, glut ourselves,

"Too much of anything, we have discovered, can **weigh** us down. Each of us needs to **fast** from something to bring ourselves to the **summit** of our **spiritual** powers."

Sister Joan Chittister

without limit, without end, with the useless and the disturbing."

In his suggestions for Lent, Benedict urges his followers toward self-denial that remembers their individual humanity. He lays down principles without imposing regulations. "During these days, therefore, we will add to the usual measure of our service something by way of private prayer and abstinence from food or drink, so that each of us will have something above the assigned measure to offer God of our own will with the joy of the Holy Spirit." Benedict's message here stresses that fasting is not a substitute for service to others; it is not a call to turn inward. And it is a matter of individual choice and responsibility, not simply a response to required behavior.

Benedict also indicates ways to avoid self-centered asceticism—fasting for fasting's sake. He recommends to monastics that they depend on a voice of wisdom—in those days that would have been the abbot or abbess—to restrain any self-destructive asceticism or misguided effort. Chittister writes: "It is so easy to ply extremes and miss the river of tradition."

"It is so easy to ply **extremes** and **miss** the **river** of **tradition.**"

Sister Joan Chittister

exploring a great spiritual practice

chapter four

Christianity
The Second
Thousand Years

At the end of the first millennium, Christianity was still a unified religion; the Catholic and Orthodox churches had not yet divided and the Protestant challenges were hundreds of years in the future. Monks and nuns were the exemplars of a dedicated Christian life. They prayed, worked, and fasted, following, by and large, the Rule of Benedict.

Ordinary Christians also fasted. For most of them, fasting remained what it had become in early Christianity: a required practice and an expression of their religious identity. Fasting on Fridays and during Lent was what Christians did. Peasant or nobility, the practice was binding. Caroline Walker Bynum tells the story of a prominent medieval family whose son left home for adventure in the East. When he returned, he was welcomed back—until he insisted on eating meat on Friday. Then the family threw him out. Bynum says, "To violate the Friday fast was the clearest, most visible way of rejecting the faith." (In this story we can also see an excellent example of the way "fast" came to be understood as abstinence from meat.)

Much changed during the ensuing thousand years. In this chapter, we search for wisdom about fasting along three Christian paths—in the Roman Catholic tradition, the Eastern Orthodox churches, and the Protestant churches. There is clearly a shared belief and a common early history, but the paths diverge. By the year 2000, wide differences in the practice of fasting had developed. We have the benefit of gathering wisdom from all three paths.

Roman Catholic tradition

As the Middle Ages advanced, we notice several conflicting and overlapping trends in Catholic spirituality of the era.

◆ Observation of the Lenten fast continued, but the requirements for both fasting and abstinence were eased.

They also became more codified. Rules and legal distinctions, exemptions and dispensations multiplied.

◆ Hypocrisy was widespread. The disparity between the Christian ideal of fasting and the way it was often practiced did not escape the sharp pen of Geoffrey Chaucer. In Canterbury Tales, his satiric wit captures the image of portly unkempt friars who boast about their tidy habits and their fasting: "Whoso would pray, he must fast and be clean, Fatten his soul and keep his body lean . . . The cleanness and the fasting of us friars result in Christ's accepting all our prayers."

◆ The emphasis on rules and on the physical aspects of fasting caused a deepening concern for the spiritual and moral dimension. Alan of Lille, a Cistercian monk writing the twelfth century, asks: "For what can it profit if the mouth rejects food while the tongue lapses into mendacity?"

"Whoso would pray, he must fast and be clean, Fatten his soul and keep his body lean ... The cleanness and the fasting of us friars Result in Christ's accepting all our prayers."

The Summoner's Tale

◆ The twelfth and thirteenth centuries brought increasing numbers of women mystics. These women, engaging in extreme ascetic practices, combined fasting with a deep reverence for a suffering Christ and their devotion to the Eucharist. Their intense experiences, while dangerously austere, drew attention to the essential link between the physical and the mystical. Contemporary feminist scholars see another dimension to this fasting. It was an opportunity, they say, for women living in an era of totally male-dominated spirituality to assert control over their own bodies and souls.

◆ For many spiritual guides, moderation became a key virtue. The thirteenth century Franciscan friar, Bonaventure, wrote: "Nor should you believe in any way that it is a greater virtue to abstain from food than to make use of food in moderation." At the same time, new and more rigorous monastic orders took root in an effort to purge lenient practices of the times.

◆ Like Bonaventure, Thomas Aquinas also believed in moderation. The revered Dominican, who was a colleague and friend of Bonaventure's, reviewed the topic of fasting in the *Summa Theologiae*, his most famous theological work. He places his analysis of abstinence and fasting within his study of the virtue of temperance; he asks why—and if—these two practices are virtues. And he answers that fasting and abstinence in themselves are "indifferent," neither virtues nor virtuous acts. The presence of what Thomas calls "right reason" makes these neutral acts virtuous: "In abstaining from food a man should act with due regard for those among whom he lives, for his own person, and for the requirements of health. . . . right reason makes one abstain as one ought, i.e. with gladness of heart, and for the due end, i.e. for God's glory and not one's own."

◆ But we also find conflicting messages in Thomas Aquinas. He praises "right reason" and "gladness of heart," but also gives—in minute detail—all the regulations for fasting: the hours for eating, the meats from which one must abstain, those who must fast and those who are dispensed (children, the elderly, pilgrims, and beggars.) His clarity about the rules may have been a necessary antidote for the confusing times, but all the legalities stripped the practice of a spiritual dimension. Aquinas also reflects his era when he gives as one of the reasons for fasting "in order to bridle the lusts of the flesh."

In the centuries that followed, history changed the face of Catholicism. But the practice of fasting for the ordinary Catholic remained remarkably static. Despite increasing laxity and, eventually, indifference, the rules and the emphasis on curbing bodily passions remained in place.

We get a glimpse of this mindset—and the arcane rules—in the Catholic Encyclopedia of 1913. There we read:

- ◆ "Moralists are one in maintaining that a natural law inculcates the necessity of fasting because every rational creature is bound to labor intelligently for the subjugation of concupiscence."

- ◆ Fasting "essentially consists in eating but one full meal in twenty-four hours and that about midday. [Fasting] also implies the obligation of abstaining from flesh meat during the same period unless legitimate authority grants permission to eat meat."

The entry describes numerous guidelines for when the main meal should be eaten (at noon), how long an interruption may last (one-half hour lest it become two meals), and the length of time the meal may last (two hours). Similarly painstaking regulations dictate the amount and kinds of food allowed. "Besides a complete meal, the Church now permits a collation usually taken in the evening. . . . about eight ounces of food are permitted at the collation. . . . Finally a little tea, coffee, chocolate or such like beverage together with a morsel of bread or a cracker is now allowed in the morning."

In mid-twentieth-century America, many of the regulations described in the Encyclopedia were still intact.

"You shall observe the prescribed days of fasting and abstinence" was one of the precepts of the church. It still is, but then the rules were stricter and more Catholics followed them. A sense of "being Catholic," of corporate identity, emerged from shared stories of tuna casseroles and snack-less dates, but fasting and abstinence were hardly sources of spiritual sustenance and, for the majority of Catholics, had little connection with the Gospel. In most Catholic parishes, Lenten sermons simply rehearsed the rules. Fasting had become religious gymnastics, the kind of spiritual activity that most Catholics now reject.

It was clearly time for a change and in 1966, Pope Paul VI, writing in an Apostolic Constitution, *Paenitemini*, undertook to establish continuity with the roots of fasting and also to explain necessary changes in the tradition: "Liturgical texts and writers of all ages clearly show the intimate bond between the external act of penance and the

"Liturgical texts and writers of all ages clearly show the intimate **bond** between the external act of **penance** and the conversion of the **soul** to **God,** through the intercession of **prayer** and **works** of **charity."**

Pope Paul VI

conversion of the soul to God, through the intercession of prayer and works of charity."

Unfortunately, the message that many Catholics heard was, "No more rules." Only in recent years have some Catholics tried to see beyond the minimal rules now in place and reclaim their spiritual legacy of fasting, touching back to the gospel message, early Church traditions, and the best of the monastic heritage. (See chapter 8.)

Eastern Orthodox Churches

The Eastern churches, although of numerous national origins, have a common spirituality. It is a spirituality solidly rooted in early Christianity, which they share with Roman Catholics and Protestants, but with a distinctly eastern perspective. Even before the split between the Roman church and the Orthodox in 1054, Orthodox spirituality had a decidedly mystical emphasis.

According to Orthodox belief, human beings, all human beings, are images, icons, of God; we are "flesh and blood images of the spiritual energy of God." The goal of every Christian life is divinization, actual participation in divine life, even here on earth. Sin is what separates human beings from this sharing in God's life and a Christian's task, therefore, is to moderate, tame, and transform human nature in order to experience God's presence.

Gregory Palamas, a fourteenth-century Orthodox monk and mystical theologian, wrote: "Indeed, only this is impossible to God, to enter into union with man before he has been cleansed." Fasting is a practice, the Orthodox believe, that cleanses their minds and bodies to prepare themselves for union with God.

What wisdom can we draw from their teachings?

◆ The human person is not evil; the body is not to be punished. Eastern Christians see repentance as a way of restoring spiritual health. Fasting is not a negative practice that simply avoids certain foods, but a liberating practice that reorients the human will and transforms human nature.

◆ Fasting is a way to move toward God, toward all that is good in creation. Bishop Kallistos (Timothy Ware) writes: "Evil resides not in created things as such, but in our attitude towards them, that is, our will. The purpose of fasting, then, is not to repudiate the divine creation but to cleanse our will."

"**Evil** resides not in created things as such, but in our **attitude** towards them, that is, our will. The purpose of **fasting,** then, is not to repudiate the **divine** creation but to **cleanse** our **will.**"

Bishop Kallistos

◆ A Russian Orthodox saying goes: "One can be damned alone, but saved only with others." Fasting for Eastern Christians is a corporate act. They fast together just as they feast together. The wisdom of the church is a collective treasure not to be lightly overturned by individual impulses. The faithful are not "to invent special rules" for themselves, but to follow "the accepted pattern" set before them.

The "accepted pattern" of fasting that is set before Eastern Christians has not varied much over the centuries and it is indeed rigorous. Church regulations suggest 180 days of fasting throughout the year. That includes most Wednesdays and Fridays, seven weeks before Easter, which the Orthodox call *Pascha*, six weeks before Christmas, and two shorter periods during the summer months.

Frederica Mathewes-Green, a popular spiritual writer and the wife of an Orthodox priest, describes it well: "For us, fasting means abstaining from certain foods: meat, fish, dairy, alcoholic beverages and olive oil (some say all oils). Oatmeal for breakfast, spaghetti marinara for dinner, and a peanut butter sandwich for lunch. Over and over again."

Orthodox regulations allow for necessary exceptions, for those who are ill, elderly, pregnant or nursing. But the teachings do not have much patience with modern rule-bending. Nor do church leaders speak kindly of the reasoning that regards fasting from food as less important than other moral practices. One contemporary Orthodox bishop, Bishop Chrysostomos, has written: "If we cannot control our tongues while fasting, our fasting is indeed useless. But if we cannot come to control our appetites and hold to a simple fast, how can we eventually overcome the temptation to judge and condemn others and succeed at the formidable task of controlling our tongues?"

Despite such clear teachings and firm leadership, the practice of fasting among contemporary believers has declined in Eastern Christian churches, as it has in Roman Catholicism and in mainline Protestant churches. And for many Orthodox believers that is a loss not only for them but also for the wider world.

"If we cannot come to **control** our **appetites** and hold to a simple **fast,** how can we eventually overcome the **temptation** to judge and condemn others and succeed at the formidable task of **controlling** our **tongues?"**

Bishop Chrysostomos

Protestant Churches

Mainline churches. Protestant Christianity began in the sixteenth century with a variety of challenges to the Roman Catholic Church. While there certainly were political, economic, and societal reasons for the Protestant Reformation, the Reformers saw themselves—primarily and quite literally—as "reformers." They wanted to reform the abuses they saw in Christianity of that era. As the century unfolded, and the Roman Catholic Church reacted by reaffirming its doctrines and practices, reform led instead to the establishment of new Christian churches. Martin Luther's objections led to Lutheranism; John Calvin's to Presbyterianism; John Wesley's to Methodism. For each of these three men, fasting was an important issue. Briefly, let us look at how the tradition of fasting came through the following centuries in each of these churches.

◆ Martin Luther wrote extensively about fasting, accepting it as an "exercise of the flesh" that helped to control the passions, but objecting to any external rules about when and how one should fast. In preaching moderation and decrying extreme asceticism that destroyed the body, he was reacting to the abuses he saw in his day. He thought that the mortifications of the time led to a false sense of confidence in behavior rather than trust in the message of the gospels. Justification was to come solely through Jesus Christ.

Luther did not believe fasting was a meritorious practice in and of itself and he did not believe any church had the authority to impose the practice on others. Lutheranism does not, therefore, issue any fasting regulations, but leaves the decision to the individual and fasting is not widely observed. Today, some Lutherans do fast, not from particular foods, but from other behaviors like gossip or over-consumption.Contemporary Lutherans have also fasted as part of peace and justice actions.

Martin **Luther's** objections led to Lutheranism; John **Calvin's** to Presbyterianism; John **Wesley's** to Methodism. For each of these three men, **fasting** was an important issue.

◆ John Calvin, in some ways, followed a more moderate ground, accepting other reasons for fasting: as a way to encourage prayer and to humble oneself before God. But, in fact, Calvin, so opposed to the hypocrisy and illusion and artificial obligations he saw in contemporary practices, did not recommend to his followers any specific corporate or individual fasting.

Fasting is not a regular part of Presbyterian practice today, but some congregations have undertaken fasting for particular reasons, such as a search for a new pastor or the future of a particular ministry.

◆ John Wesley also objected to the abuses of his day, but he both believed in and practiced fasting. His pattern of fasting was to follow a weekly regimen: he did not eat after his Thursday evening meal until mid-afternoon on Friday. During this time he ate no solid foods and devoted himself to prayer.

Methodists are encouraged to follow Wesley's example year-round, but if that is not possible, at least during weeks between Easter and Pentecost. The importance, Methodist leaders say, is not the specific details of how and when, but participating with other believers and understanding the reasons for fasting.

In addition to these three mainline Protestant churches, we can look to the Anglican Church, which also traces its roots to the sixteenth century, for historical insights into fasting. In the Anglican Communion, which includes the Episcopal Church of America, *The Book of Common Prayer* once included many dates for fasting, but left the observance to individual conscience. The list of suggested fast days actually resembled an old Roman Catholic calendar; it included all Fridays, the days of Lent, Rogation Days, quarterly Ember Days, and the vigils of certain feasts. But even in nineteenth-century England, when Edward Pusey and John Henry Newman both wrote in defense of fasting, there was little interest in the practice. Today, the list of fast days has disappeared, observance of the practice is still left to the discretion of the individual, and few Anglicans fast.

Mormon church. The Prophet Joseph Smith, who founded the Church of Jesus Christ of Latter-Day Saints in 1830, heard in a revelation that the Lord commanded the Latter-Day Saints to "continue in prayer and fasting from this time forward."

The practice is part of every Mormon's life and is described in the Mormon General Handbook of Instructions: "A proper fast-day observance consists of abstaining from food and drink for two consecutive meals, attending the fast and testimony meeting, and making a generous offering to the bishop for the care of those in need. A minimum fast offering is defined as the equivalent of two meals."

Church members generally fast together on the first Sunday of each month. There is an emphasis, Mormons say, on making this twenty-four-hour period a deeply spiritual experience. At the Sunday Fast and Testimony Meeting, members of the church witness to their beliefs in Jesus Christ and break their fast by participating in the sacrament of the Lord's Supper. Their fast offerings, which may be cash or in-kind donations, are given to the bishop to care for the needy.

Evangelical churches. For evangelical Christians, the Bible is an essential sacred text and Bible study an important spiritual discipline. Until recently, however, despite the biblical references to fasting, the practice had not been a part of the everyday life of evangelical Christians. That changed in the early 1990s as several American evangelical leaders rediscovered fasting as a companion to prayer and preached its importance to their followers. This modern reinvigoration of fasting has reached hundreds of thousands, perhaps millions, of evangelical Christians, who have attended conferences, bought motivational books, and started fasting crusades in their own hometown churches. (See chapter 11 for an extensive look at the resurgence of fasting in evangelical churches.)

This brief historical review shows that at the end of the second millennium, with the exception of the Mormons and evangelical Christians, fasting has declined in the lives of most contemporary Christians. The large majority views the practice with indifference or even distaste. That presents a challenge for some contemporary spiritual seekers: Is fasting in a Christian context fatally irrelevant today? Or are there ways Christians can reclaim their gospel legacy and give an ancient spiritual practice contemporary significance? We'll come back to these questions in the second part of the book.

exploring a great spiritual practice

chapterfive

Islam

Muslims locate the roots of their faith and their spirituality in the life of Mohammad, known as the Prophet, and in the *Qur'an* (or Koran), the sacred text that contains the word of God as it was revealed to the Prophet. Fasting played a large role in the life of the Prophet; it is also mandated in the *Qur'an* for all faithful followers of Islam.

Mohammad, a descendant of Ishmael, son of Abraham, the Hebrew patriarch, lived during the sixth and seventh centuries in what is now Saudi Arabia. His revelations from God, which took place over a twenty-three-year period in his life, began when he was forty and praying alone in a cave during a retreat he made each year during the month of Ramadan.

In the years that followed, Mohammad preached Islam, belief in one God, in the city of Mecca which was awash in

"The various ways that **God** provides sustenance for people and animals are 'signs' of **His** existence that should cause the thoughtful person to **believe** in **Him** and be **grateful.**"

Valerie J. Hoffman

the worship of many gods. He and his followers were severely persecuted and in 622 the Prophet fled from Mecca to Medina. This famous flight (or *hegira*) marked a dramatic change in the Prophet's life and in the development of Islam. Fasting during Ramadan, the sacred month when the *Qur'an* was first revealed to the Prophet, became obligatory for Muslims shortly after the *hegira*.

It is important to place our observations about the Prophet and the *Qur'an* in context. The Prophet fasted often and for long periods of time, yet, like the desert monks of early Christianity, he also spoke frequently of moderation and of the importance of love and hospitality. The *Qur'an* expects fasting, but it also speaks of feasting. A significant theme throughout the teachings of Islam, reminiscent of themes we found in Judaism, is God's love for humanity. Valerie J. Hoffman writes that in Islam, "the various ways that God provides sustenance for people and animals are 'signs' of His existence that should cause the thoughtful person to believe in Him and be grateful."

The Five Pillars of Islam

As Mohammad built his new community after the *hegira*, complex codes of behavior, revealed in the sacred *Qur'an*, regulated the lives of the early followers of Islam. The *Qur'an* dictated five essential religious duties, generally known as the Five Pillars of Islam, that still govern the lives of faithful Muslims today, wherever they have settled.

The five pillars or practices, while specific to Islam, will not be unfamiliar to spiritual seekers of many religious backgrounds. First among them is a profession of faith. Muslims must assent to their basic creed: "There is no god but Allah and Muhammad is his prophet." Prayer is the second obligation; Muslims must pray five times a day. The third required spiritual practice is fasting; Muslims must fast from  daybreak to dark every day during Ramadan, the ninth month of the lunar calendar. The fourth is almsgiving, sometimes viewed as a religious tax, an obligation that assists the poor and should remind the giver of God's goodness. The final pillar is pilgrimage—the well-known *hajj*. All healthy Muslims must travel to Mecca, Islam's holiest site, at least once in their lives.

Fasting in the Qur'an

The *Qur'an*, scholars say, is the source of all that is Islamic. It is the Word of God, as Mohammad heard it in Arabic from the mouth of the archangel Gabriel. And thus all of the *Qur'an*—its sound, form, and meaning—is sacred. Here are the words from *sura* (or chapter) two that describe a Muslim's obligation to fast:

O believers! A Fast is prescribed to you as it was prescribed to those before you, that you may fear God,

For certain days. But he among you who shall be sick, or on a journey, shall fast that same number of other days: and as for those who are able to keep it and yet break it, the expiation of this shall be the maintenance of a poor man. And he who of his own accord performs a good work, shall derive good from it: and good shall it be for you to fast—if you knew it.

As to the month Ramadhan in which the Koran was sent down to be man's guidance . . . as soon as any one of you observes the moon, let him set about the fast; but he who is sick or upon a journey shall fast a like number of other days. God wishes you ease, but wishes not your discomfort. . . .

You are allowed on the night of the fast to approach your wives . . . eat and drink until you can discern a white thread from a black thread by the daybreak: then fast strictly till night and go not in unto them, but rather pass the time in mosques.

What can we learn from this text?

◆ Fasting during Ramadan is expected, but those who are sick or traveling may substitute fasting on other days. Islam teaches that pregnant or nursing women are also exempt. In theory, a Muslim can compensate for not fasting during Ramadan by donating money to feed the poor, but in practice, Muslims say, this is seldom done.

◆ Fasting curbs several appetites. In this text, fasting means abstaining from food, drink, and sexual intercourse during the daylight hours of Ramadan.

◆ While the fast is strict, God is kind and merciful. Islam's Allah does not place extraordinary

"People who have **fasted** for **twenty-nine days** within the **year** will be apt to **listen** more carefully when next approached by **someone** who is **hungry.**"

difficulties in people's lives. As the *Qur'an* says: "God wishes you ease."

Fasting in Islam, like all of the other Five Pillars, has both an external and an internal dimension. The external rules—fasting for the body—are clear from the passage. But there is more—fasting for the soul. The Prophet says, "Cultivate within yourselves the Attributes of God." Those who do not eat, drink, or have sex during a specified time such as Ramadan can strengthen themselves to imitate the qualities of God—to become more truthful, less angry, more loving. Those who fast and still engage in morally offensive behavior are not truly fasting. The Prophet says, "There are many whose fasting is nothing beyond being hungry and thirsty."

Fasting during Ramadan should also make Muslims more sensitive to the struggles of those who are poor and hungry. Huston Smith writes: "People who have fasted for twenty-nine days within the year will be apt to listen more carefully when next approached by someone who is hungry."

Fasting in the Life of the Prophet

In the *Qur'an,* Muslims believe they have God's words, spoken directly to Mohammad, the last of the great prophets. But the sacred text is not history or biography, and so we must turn to other Islamic sources to learn about the life of the Prophet. In the *hadith,* a collection of thousands of Mohammad's words and actions, we are given, in his own words, not God's, the Prophet's spiritual wisdom, his theological insights, and his instructions for all manner of daily rituals. From the *hadith* we can also glimpse the character of the man Muslims revere as God's Messenger. We are told what Mohammad ate and even what his favorite foods were. Clearly, he had strong appetites. But we also learn about his frequent personal fasts and his attitudes toward fasting.

◆ One *hadith* tells the story of three men who criticized the Prophet's spiritual observances, comparing his to their own more rigorous practices of prayer, fasting, and celibacy. Mohammad rebukes them: "I dread God more than you and revere him more, but I fast and I break the fast; I pray and I sleep, too, and I marry women."

◆ In another, the Prophet describes the best fast as "one that is regularly broken so that the body would not suffer ill-health nor become so accustomed to fasting that it no longer feels hunger."

◆ Once, the story goes, the Prophet confronted a close companion who was following a severe fasting regimen. The Prophet asked: "Have you not in me an example?" When the man agreed, Mohammad told him to stop fasting every day and keeping vigil every night. "Verily your eyes have their rights over you, and your body has its rights, and your family has their rights. So pray, and sleep, and fast, and break fast."

The Prophet taught that moderation was a key element of spirituality. His followers were to fast, yes, but they were also to balance self-denial with enjoyment of God-given natural pleasures.

Wisdom from the Sufi Tradition

Sufism is the mystical dimension of Islam. Despite some recent controversy about its pedigree and the presence of outside influences, Sufism is deeply rooted in both the *Qur'an* and the life of the Prophet. The Sufi practice the Five Pillars of Islam, but also have a deep awareness of the internal struggle of the soul to surrender to God ("the greater *jihad*"). A *Qur'anic* verse reads: "From God we came and to God shall we return." The Sufi path is a journey back to God.

The Sufi trace their heritage to the Prophet and an oral "chain of transmission" that led from Mohammad to his companions and followers to later Sufi masters to present day Sufi. The core practices are prayer, meditation, fasting, and other acts of self-discipline. As in the Jewish and Christian mystical traditions, severe ascetical practices have been a part of Sufism, particularly in its early development during the eighth and ninth centuries. But, as we search for the core of Sufi wisdom on fasting, we turn to the voice of the man who is the master of moderate Sufism, Al-Ghazzali (Abu-Hamid Muhammad Al-Ghazzali), a theologian and philosopher who lived in what is now Iran from 1058 to 1111.

Al-Ghazzali, who had studied Christian and Greek classics, came to believe that love was the essence of religion. He abandoned his own academic career for the Sufi spiritual path, but his scholarly gifts brought Sufism back from the edges of Islamic practice.

"**Fasting** is a tool for training and **subduing** the **soul**, opening the spirit to God. . . . But **eating** and **drinking** can also be **sacred** acts, conveying spiritual power and blessing."

Valerie J. Hoffman

Because the Sufi follow the example of the Prophet as well as the laws in the *Qur'an*, Al-Ghazzali quoted frequently from both the *Qur'an* and the *hadith*. He believed in the central importance of fasting for the spiritual life, but, following the example of the Prophet, he also preached moderation. Fasting was important, but so were hospitality and expressing one's love for others.

◆ He wrote: "If it makes your brother happy for you to break your fast, you should break it, and your reward is greater than the reward of your fast, if your intention is to make your brother happy."

◆ He quoted a cousin of the Prophet: "One of the best good deeds is to honor those with whom you are sitting by breaking the fast. Breaking the fast with this intention is an act of worship and good etiquette, and its reward is greater than the reward of fasting."

In the Sufi tradition, as in Islam itself, fasting is an essential spiritual discipline. It curbs physical appetites and strengthens the soul in humility, patience, and gratitude—virtues necessary for anyone who seeks union with God. But, the Sufi say, fasting cannot be separated from love—from love of a God who showers blessings, including food, on his creatures or from love of one's companions and neighbors. Abstinence alone is not sufficient to reach the divine goal that lies at the end of the spiritual path.

Valerie J. Hoffman sums up the Sufi attitude: "Fasting is a tool for training and subduing the soul, opening the spirit to God. . . . But eating and drinking can also be sacred acts, conveying spiritual power and blessing." This attitude is deeply rooted in Islam, but contains clear similarities to other religious traditions.

exploring a great spiritual practice

chaptersix

More Traditions from the East and West

Fasting has played a role in many other cultures and religions—in ancient Egypt; in Greece among the Cynics, the Stoics, and at the shrines of the oracles; in indigenous American, African, and Australian cultures; in pre-Christian Iceland; in Hinduism, Buddhism, Confucianism, and Taoism.

Among these cultures and religions, fasting came in all guises. It was an ascetic practice to punish the body and achieve self-control or to free the soul and achieve inner peace; it was part of a penitential rite that showed sorrow for misdeeds and thus staved off the anger and punishment of a divine being; it accompanied requests for favor from a deity;

it preceded—and perhaps caused—a vision or a dream that provided wisdom for the future; it was required as preparation for service as a seer, shaman, healer, or oracle.

In our search for wisdom to apply to contemporary fasting, we select three traditions from this rich history and global backdrop. From the East, we draw from Hinduism and Buddhism and from the West, from Native American spirituality.

Hinduism

The heart of Hinduism, an ancient religion that traces its roots to India three millennia ago, is a search for higher consciousness among human beings. How can human beings come into contact, and stay in contact, with Brahman (God)? Seeking inner transformation is the foundational purpose of the Hindu spiritual path. One must leave behind pleasure, the quest for knowledge, and the obligation of civic duty in order to concentrate on what Hindus call enlightenment.

Depending on one's personality, there are in Hinduism differing *yogas* or paths toward enlightenment, but all begin with moral practices common to many other religions. Like devout Jews, Christians, and Muslims, Hindus believe that self-centered behavior gets in the way of spiritual progress. Moral behavior is essential for advancing along the path to enlightenment. So spiritual seekers among the Hindus esteem truthfulness, nonviolence, cleanliness, and self-control. Many Hindus are vegetarian; they do not believe in killing animals and hold cows to be sacred. Bathing or cleansing is a part of many rituals, and fasting is, for most Hindus, a significant practice.

In fact, few Hindu rituals or festivals are not accompanied by fasting; in some lunar months there as many as ten fast days. Hindu tradition attaches special intentions to many of these fast days. One fasts, for example, for the protection of children, for prosperity, for human fertility. All Hindus are expected, health permitting, to fast, and women are among the most faithful of Hindu fasters. They fast frequently throughout the year for reasons such as the long life of their husbands, to nullify the effects of "menstrual pollution," and for marital fidelity.

To bring the practice of fasting among Hindus into clearer focus, we now look in depth at two areas: fasting among women and the fasting practiced by Mohandas Gandhi.

Hindu women. The practice of fasting has been part of the life of Hindu women for millennia. It is a ritual kind of fasting, usually called a *vrat* or vow, which includes other components, such as worship and the giving of gifts. Throughout India, today's Hindu women—regardless of age, wealth, education, or caste—still observe *vrats*. We can ask two questions.

First of all, why? Hindu women give many answers.

◆ Fasting is a duty, a way of ordering their lives, and a practice they learned from their mothers. But it is also optional; the women choose to fast—and they choose which *vrats* to follow.

◆ The practice helps them alter their behavior and discipline themselves so that they advance along the path to enlightenment. Their fasting is just one part of a religious act, which usually includes *puja* or worship to a particular deity, meditation, and the giving of gifts, which may be food or money.

◆ Whatever the specific intention attached to a *vrat*, each ritual should also lead to deeper contentment and purification of the heart. It is important, Hindu women say, to understand that they are not bargaining for favors. Fasting is a gift of self. Their faith, however, tells them that keeping a *vrat* will achieve the benefits they desire.

♦ Fasting is good for one's health.

♦ Fasting allows them to exert some control over their lives in a culture where women's roles traditionally are submissive. In this motive, they are not unlike some medieval women, the Christian mystics who used their austerities to assert some personal control over their spiritual (and physical) lives.

Hindu fasting thus blends moral, ethical, and personal motives with spiritual objectives. Our second question is: What does Hindu fasting look like? Hindu fasting does not impose universal rules; the emphasis remains on the individual's self-gift. Indian women's practices give us glimpses into the many variations of Hindu fasting.

♦ Fasts can last twenty-four hours or longer. They can require eating only after sundown or only one meal a day. There are annual fasts in honor of

The practice of **fasting** has been part of the life of **Hindu** women for millennia. It is a ritual kind of fasting, usually called a *vrat* or **VOW**, which includes other components, such as **worship** and the giving of **gifts**.

specific deities, monthly lunar fasts, and fasts before special occasions, such as marriage.

◆ Total abstention from food may be the ideal, but practices vary. More frequently, the Hindu faster restricts the quantity and the kinds of food that may be eaten. Most fasts require abstaining from meat. Some also ban salt and grain products, such as rice, lentils, and barley. Some may allow fruits (such as bananas, plums, or water chestnuts) and dairy products. The food allowed is usually the kind that purifies and cleanses the body.

◆ The days before and after the fast are also sacred days. During the fast, one refrains from an act of violence toward any creature (hence the abstention from meat). *Ahimsa* (or nonviolence) has become one of the most important "exports" of Indian religious practice.

Mohandas Gandhi. The man who became known to the world as a model of nonviolent political action, who used personal fasting as a powerful public statement, learned how to fast from a Hindu woman: his mother.

In the first chapter of his autobiography, *My Experiments with Truth,* Gandhi speaks with admiration of his mother's religious practices. "The outstanding impression my mother has left on my memory is that of saintliness. She was deeply religious. She would not think of taking her meals without her daily prayers. . . . She would take the hardest vows and keep them without flinching. . . . To keep two or three consecutive fasts was nothing to her."

The autobiography makes clear that the two principles that motivated Gandhi were the basic Hindu principles of Truth and *ahimsa*. Gandhi was always striving "to see God face to face." The God he worshipped was Truth, and Gandhi believed that a truth-seeker must follow a narrow path, being "humbler than dust." Thus, he describes his practices as "experiments" where there is no room for self-praise. The title of "Mahatma" or Great Soul, which others gave him, made him uncomfortable.

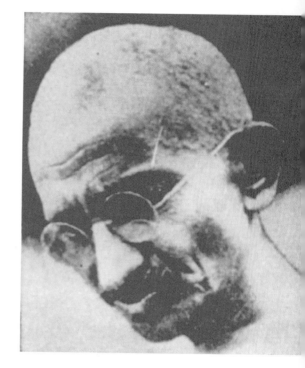

According to Gandhi, *ahimsa* meant nonviolence. "But to me," he said, "it has much higher, infinitely higher meaning. It means that you may not offend anybody; you may not harbor uncharitable thought, even in connection with those you consider your enemies."

Gandhi's early public fasts were not political but penitential. Twice he fasted to atone for the misbehavior of young students in his care in South Africa. Even in these early episodes, Gandhi combined the public act of fasting with private spiritual motives. He viewed his fasts as ways to harness his passions and make himself fit for the struggle toward Truth as well as tools to achieve, nonviolently, other political objectives.

Gandhi returned to India in 1915 and for more than thirty years he played a role, often reluctantly, in Indian politics. He fasted in sympathy with striking mill workers, for the improved status of the untouchables, and in opposition to British control of India. As India moved toward independence, Gandhi's devotion to Truth and *ahimsa*, with fasting as an essential element, became revered around the world as a model for nonviolent political action.

Gandhi's practice of fasting brought dramatic historical results. But from his life and writings we can also draw some insights into personal fasting.

◆ Physical fasting is important, but it alone is not sufficient. The moral or spiritual element of fasting is essential.

◆ Gandhi believed that all his acts, including fasting, had to remain true to his reason and his heart. He carefully studied his own psychological makeup and was scrupulous in assessing his own strengths and weaknesses.

◆ Gandhi would not prescribe a spiritual path for anyone else. His own fasts sometimes lasted as long as three weeks, but he never asked anyone to fast with him for more than a day.

What we see in Gandhi is the kind of fasting that is not motivated by a set of rules or by fear of punishment. It is not imposed by others, but freely undertaken for a variety of reasons, all of which reflect a person's own heart.

Buddhism

While Hinduism developed slowly over many centuries, Buddhism came into existence during the lifetime of one man, Siddartha Gautama, who lived from around 563 to 483 B.C.E., and who became known as the Buddha, the Enlightened One. In many ways, Buddhism was a reaction to the Hinduism of that time, which had become authoritarian, exploitative, and mired in superstition. The Buddha had searched for life's meaning as a good Hindu, had studied with many *yogis*, and fasted so strenuously that, as he described it, "when I thought I would touch the skin of my stomach I actually took hold of my spine." But searching, studying, and rigorous fasting did not bring enlightenment. Only when at last he gave up fasting, did enlightenment come.

And there the Buddha found the beginning of his teachings: what has been called the Middle Way, which leads a believer between the temptations of the pleasurable life and extreme asceticism to a balance of the physical and spiritual. The Middle Way, the fourth of the Buddha's Noble Truths, is actually a course of action and is also known as the Eightfold

Path. By attempting to follow these eight practices throughout their lives Buddhists train themselves in right behavior. Right behavior leads to a calm and peaceful mind.

Over the centuries, the teachings of the Buddha have been interpreted differently by a variety of schools and traditions. For many Buddhists, the Middle Way means that restraint is more important than abstinence, but for others, right fasting remains a part of their practice.

Theravada Buddhists, for example, revere the spiritual path followed by monks and nuns, who traditionally eat only one meal a day. In recent years, as this branch of Buddhism has reached Europe and the United States, monasteries and meditation centers have welcomed lay people to join the monastics and share in their lifestyle for a specific period of time. The Theravada practice of fasting from noon until the next morning has thus become more widespread. (See page 00 for more information about Theravada Buddhist monasteries and retreat centers.) Lay Buddhists may also fast in this monastic style on holy days or full moon days, not eating from noon until the following sunrise. Liquids, such as tea and juices, are usually allowed. Other Buddhists observe holy days with dawn to dusk fasts. In addition, many Buddhists interpret *ahimsa,* or harmlessness, the first of the precepts or ethical guidelines of their religion, as prohibiting all killing, even of animals, and are thus strict vegetarians.

For those who follow the teachings of the Buddha, fasting is prudent, moral, ethical, and self-imposed. There are two threads in Buddhist teaching that contemporary spiritual seekers might find particularly helpful.

◆ Buddhism, like Hinduism, values *ahimsa*. Fasting has often been part of the Buddhist witness to non-violence and the fasting practices of Buddhist monastics during the anti-Vietnam War movement became a model for many westerners. Fasting can teach us to respect the value of other lives, human or not; it can strengthen our connections to the rest of the world; it can aid our mindfulness. These are the Buddhist values and connections we hear in the well-known voices of the Dalai Lama and Thich Nhat Hahn.

◆ The Buddha recognized the importance of "right association." As we seek enlightenment, we can benefit from good example. By associating with and imitating those whose spirit we see as holy, we can make progress along the Way.

Native American Spirituality

There are many similarities between Eastern religions and Native American spirituality. Native Americans also believe in the essential link between our physical and spiritual selves. A Sioux medicine man describes healing as helping a person be in touch with the Spirit. As in Hinduism and Buddhism, inner transformation of both the individual and the community are vital to the well being of a society.

Each of us must strive to live in harmony within ourselves, with each other, and with the Spirit.

In Native American cultures, fasting was widespread. It was both a solitary practice and a communal effort and provided a way of getting in touch with spirits who offered protection or guidance. Probably the most well-known example of the solitary kind of fasting is the vision quest, in which a young man was sent off into the wilderness to fast and wait for a dream or vision that would reveal to him something about his future.

Fasting in a communal setting preceded or accompanied sacred rituals, such as the Sun Dance, and prepared tribal members to receive guidance from the Great Spirit. When fasting accompanied rituals where, for instance, a tribe prayed for fertility or a good harvest, ceremonial requirements dictated the length and kind of fasting. Many Native American tribes also used sweat lodges where members spent hours, even days, undergoing the rigors of intense heat and fasting. The practice was meant to purify participants, which would then lead to spiritual renewal and healing.

Whether undertaken alone in the wilderness or in the sweat lodge with other tribal members, fasting was a self-discipline that strengthened the body and purified an individual before a great challenge. The Cherokee, for example, believed that before one could slay an eagle, one had to undergo a long and arduous period of prayer and fasting. Most importantly, the practice was an essential element of Native American prayer; it accompanied meditation and allowed the faithful practitioner to commune with the Spirit.

Fasting was also part of the moral teachings Native American parents passed on to their children. We get a wonderful glimpse of this practical aspect of our Native American heritage in the numerous no-nonsense instructions one Winnebago father gave his son. About fasting, he said:

♦ "You ought to be of some help to your fellowmen and for that reason I counsel you to fast."

♦ "Some day you will be traveling on a road filled with obstacles and then you will wish that you had fasted. So that you will not find it necessary to blame yourself, I counsel you to fast."

♦ "Fast for food you are to receive. If you fast often enough for these things, then some day when your children ask for food, they will be able to obtain without difficulty a piece of deer meat, or perhaps even a piece of moose meat. You have it within you to see to it that your children shall never be hungry."

Fasting in Native American spirituality had clear practical ramifications. It kept the faster in touch with hunger, his own hunger and his family's; it provided inner strength to combat the hardships of life and to follow through on service to others; and it provided a way, alone or with others, to reach out to the Great Spirit—to pray and receive guidance.

During the twentieth century, much of the Native American heritage was "lost," but a welcome contemporary renewal has revitalized tribal cultures and customs, including the spiritual role of fasting. In one present day inter-tribal ceremony in Oregon, for example, Native American men participate in a traditional endurance dance, which involves both fasting and rigorous dance. Visitors are invited to bring a token of an ill relative and attach it to a dancer's ceremonial dress. The men dance what has been described as "a living prayer" for all who need healing.

As we finish our brief look at these fasting traditions from East and West, we can see an underlying universality in the practice of fasting. Some of the themes we first traced through Judaism or Christianity resurface here—in different language perhaps and with different cultural emphasis. Other aspects of the practice are unique to a particular religion or a particular historical period. Our task now is to see how wisdom from these many traditions surfaces in contemporary fasting.

Seasons
and Reasons

"Singing, dancing, even shouting characterize the disciplines of the spiritual life."

Richard J. Foster

exploring a great spiritual practice

chapter**seven**

YomKippurFasting

Yom Kippur, meaning Day of Atonement, is the most familiar—and the most universal—of the Jewish fast days. It is rooted in the Hebrew Scriptures, interpreted by rabbinic tradition, and accepted in all contemporary branches of Judaism.

Yom Kippur concludes a ten-day period of introspection that begins with the celebration of Rosh Hashanah, the first day of the Jewish New Year. For Jews, all ten days during this period, sometimes called the "Days of Awe," are holy—they are times for prayer and self-reflection. If, for example, one has offended a spouse or neighbor or coworker, this is the time to make an effort to apologize and set things right. It is also the time when many Jews give donations to charity.

Seen in this context, Yom Kippur is both the culmination of a deeply spiritual time and an intensely prayerful day in itself. On the Day of Atonement, fasting is a physical manifestation of the spiritual affliction mandated in the Torah: "On that day you shall afflict your souls. . . " (Leviticus 23:27). Rabbi David Wise, who leads a Conservative Jewish congregation, says, "On Yom Kippur, we are so focused on repentance and on confronting our misdeeds of the previous years and so committed to fixing them, we are so conscious of our mortality that we are in essence praying for our lives that day and so the last thing we worry about is food."

After a brief summary of some basic information about fasting on Yom Kippur, we will direct our attention to what the rabbis deem important: the spiritual dimensions of fasting.

The Basics

Day begins with night, the Jews say, following the description of creation in the book of Genesis. And so Shabbat, the Jewish Sabbath, and all Jewish holidays begin with sundown. Yom Kippur is considered a twenty-five-hour fast—from one sundown until the next. During that time the Talmud prescribes five restrictions: Jews must abstain from food, drink, marital intercourse, anointing with oil, and wearing leather shoes. Jews who follow the injunctions of the rabbis may not work on Yom Kippur and will usually spend a good part of the evening and the day at prayer in their synagogue or temple.

The meals before and after the Yom Kippur fast each have significance. The first has religious meaning; the second has cultural importance.

◆ In an effort to prevent extreme asceticism, rabbinic teaching has prohibited any fasting before Yom Kippur. Eating the pre-fast meal is a *mitzvah*, a religious duty; one is required to eat before embarking on the fast. Rabbi Elyse Frishman says, "The meal that precedes Yom Kippur is customarily an important meal. It's more somber than a meal before any other holiday. At every other holiday there's a special blessing you recite over wine signifying the sweetness of the day. You don't do that before Yom Kippur because it's not a sweet day. It's a profound, provocative day." But it is not a sad meal. Rabbi Wise explains, "We are commanded to be equally joyous in eating that meal as we are to be serious and self-reflective in the fasting process."

◆ No special foods are designated, but many Jews say that chicken soup with matzo balls or *kreplach* (triangular meat-filled dumplings) has long been a part of their family's traditional pre-fast meal. Contemporary Jews recommend eating lightly, instead of trying to eat for two days; and they avoid heavily spiced foods or anything that may cause them discomfort that night or the next day.

◆ Judaism is a religion with a deep sense of community, and at the end of Yom Kippur breaking the fast with family and friends is an important event. Many synagogues and temples serve a break-fast meal at the end of the Yom Kippur services. No ritual foods are required. Some congregations set out fruit and bread or cake. Others will serve more elaborate meals. The important thing, Jews say, is not to break the fast by yourself. For people who live alone, the congregation meal may be a blessing; others prefer to leave the synagogue to eat at home with family and friends.

Spiritual Dimensions

The teachings of Judaism clearly emphasize the spiritual significance of Yom Kippur fasting. Let's look at some contemporary spiritual dimensions of the practice.

◆ Prayer. Since biblical times, the Jews have recognized prayer as a valued way to communicate with God. During the twenty-five-hour Yom Kippur fast, observant Jews spend a large portion of that time in prayer. Some remain all day in the temple or synagogue. Services begin in the evening and continue the next morning and afternoon, concluding with a final evening service. The services include readings from the Hebrew Scriptures, sermons, hymns, and congregational prayers.

◆ The message is repeatedly made clear: the congregation, individually and as a group, is making atonement for sin and seeking divine forgiveness. Fasting is a way of deepening this prayer experience, of focusing the mind on communicating with God.

◆ Penitence. Rabbi Abraham Isaac Kook, Chief Rabbi of Palestine before the establishment of the State of Israel and a respected contemporary voice of Jewish mysticism, wrote, "Penitence derives from the yearning of all existence to be better, purer, firmer, nobler than it is." He believed that penitence liberated a person from remorse and brought delight. "Great is penitence for it brings healing to the world."

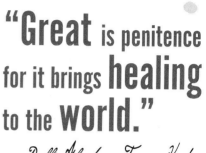

"**Great** is penitence for it brings **healing** to the **world.**"

Rabbi Abraham Isaac Kook

◆ Judaism teaches that there is a difference between penitence, rightly understood and clearly recommended, and excessive penance or asceticism, which is against Jewish law. All that God has made, including our bodies, is good and not to be abused. On Yom Kippur, the fast may be difficult, but it is within proper bounds. Fasting for the day is a communal commitment and a personal *mitzvah* that brings both joy and thanksgiving upon completion.

◆ Compassion. One of the traditional readings during morning services on Yom Kippur is the valued message of the prophet Isaiah, which we discussed in chapter 1.

Isaiah told the biblical Jews that no fasting mattered if it was not accompanied by efforts to right injustice, to feed the hungry, to remove the chains of oppression. Fasting can radically change our perceptions by allowing us to feel within our own bodies the hunger of others. But such an experience of compassion must lead outward—to action. Contributing to charity in some way is an essential component of Yom Kippur fasting.

Rabbi Frishman, who describes her Reform congregation as a "gateway" community that embraces many newcomers to Jewish practices, wants her congregation to understand the message of Isaiah. Yom Kippur, she says, is a day of profound ritual and if ritual is supposed to bring us to social action, it would be a shame to miss the opportunity "to engage the whole congregation in a specific social project. We do food drives that begin right then."

◆ Moral actions. Fasting on Yom Kippur requires self-discipline. Jews who have observed the fast for many years say it is not so much physically painful as it is a test of their endurance. Some years it requires every ounce of their will power to resist the opportunities that arise. Ours is a culture of eating; food is everywhere for the taking. The decision not to eat must be made over and over again during a single twenty-five-hour period.

◆ Yom Kippur provides a yearly opportunity for Jews to focus on changing their lives. Fasting, they say, allows them space for that introspection.

Voices

Harriet Sepinwall

I grew up in East Harlem. I was the only Jewish child in my neighborhood. On Yom Kippur I would go with my mother to a small synagogue. At lunchtime she would walk me back home so she could give me lunch, and then we would walk back to the synagogue. I think I started fasting myself when I was eleven.

I remember once, when I was about sixteen or seventeen, I passed out. It was a hot day. I was fasting, and I was in the synagogue. I remember somebody using smelling salts to arouse me. The next time I remember an issue about fasting was when I was diagnosed with hypoglycemia, and my rabbi said that Judaism does not want anyone to fast if it's going to be a punitive fast. It had to be a spiritual fast, and I had to eat.

Now that I no longer seem to have hypoglycemia, I'm back to fasting.

Before I begin the fast, I choose foods that won't be too salty to make me thirsty and that won't make me uncomfortable. I don't overeat either. I have a regular, traditional meal. I'll have a salad, chicken soup and matzo balls, chicken or meat entrée with a vegetable, and maybe a traditional potato kugel or baked potato, fruit for dessert and tea. My mother always made kreplach, *which are triangular-shaped dumplings filled with chopped meat. Do you know them? Maybe that's only a Yom Kippur tradition for Eastern European Jews.*

Fasting provides me an opportunity to spend a whole day in a synagogue focusing on changing myself, thinking about how I can become a better person. I've learned a lot about that from my Rabbi, Alan Silverstein. He says there are three themes for the High Holy Days. One is prayer. Another is tzedukah, *to make contributions or volunteer or do good works. Before Rosh Hashanah, or certainly by Yom Kippur, I make contributions to the organizations I support. Another is* t'shuvah, *to change yourself. It begins with an examination of yourself. I think about the things in the Jewish tradition that teach me how to live my life. That's part of the change; it's repentance and change. Have I done the things that I really* wanted to do, that are the right things to do, that will help make my life a better life? We're talking about very personal, deep-down things. Am I nice to strangers? Kind to family and friends? Am I ethical in my teaching? So self-examination comes first, and then I'm obligated to work on changing myself and also to make amends to others.

Fasting provides the time and the space to do this within yourself. I'll joke with my students. I'll say that if you don't have to be busy in the kitchen cooking and serving and doing the dishes, you can focus on more important things. On Yom Kippur there's no schedule of any sort except the schedule of being in synagogue and knowing that I'm going to spend my time praying to G-d, asking for help in finding ways to become a better person.

In my synagogue, we spend most of the first evening praying. I have to get there early if I want to get a seat where I can see and hear. Then in the morning we return. Services can begin as early as eight o'clock. There are prayers all morning and our rabbi gives a sermon. There's usually a break anywhere between two-thirty and three o'clock. Then you go back to synagogue at about five o'clock. Those services don't end until after sunset. That's a time when most people are tired from fasting, but more and more people in my congregation are returning to end the holy day together. We also break the fast together. We have light refreshments in the synagogue social room.

I'm very lucky. One of my great supports is my congregation, where most of us want to be on what our rabbi *calls "the ladder of commitment." Spiritually, you should be comfortable wherever you're starting on this ladder, but you should still be striving to go higher. And I have some people with whom I can talk about fasting and about what Yom Kippur means to me. They're usually other people for whom religious traditions are important, whether they're Jewish or Protestant or Catholic or Muslim. People who are not religious are not so interested, and that could include people who are Jewish. I know some people who fast as adults the same way as I fasted as a child—without really thinking about the meaning. It is just a tradition for them, something good from the past, maybe. But it is much more than that for me.*

Harriet Sepinwall is a college professor, director of a Holocaust Education Resource Center, and a member of a Conservative Jewish congregation.

Voices

Richard Cameron

I've gone through an evolution in my life. Probably since my own Bar Mitzvah I have, if not religiously observed Yom Kippur, I would say de facto observed it. Which means that I would not work, and I would fast. But I did not attend synagogue. For about twenty-five years I was not active in religious life. Once my children entered religious school, I returned to the flock. And I would say that now I am a regular Friday night participant at synagogue. I take it pretty seriously.

We have two daughters. My seventeen-year-old had a Bat Mitzvah and was Confirmed. I would say she's at the point in her life where religion is in question in her mind as it is with most [teenagers]. So her attention to ritual is considerably less than it was when she was younger. And it remains to be seen what she will do when she's older. I mean that's beyond my control. Not beyond my interest, but beyond my control. So at the moment she sort of fasts through Yom Kippur, which is the only fasting holiday Reform Jews celebrate.

My older daughter is twenty-one. She was also brought up in the Reform tradition and had a Bat Mitzvah and was also Confirmed. She's planning on applying to rabbinic school. So she is, I would say, more observant than my younger daughter. If you are planning on applying to rabbinic school, you're seriously thinking about living a Jewish life. My older daughter fasts, period.

I'm a work in progress myself. To be a work in progress is a good thing. I'm certainly growing and learning, and I am re-involving myself in my own tradition to the extent to which I feel comfortable. For me fasting on Yom Kippur is denying yourself and humbling yourself before God. It's the discipline of appearing before God in an unsated state. Maybe God will look kindly upon you for another year.

I think fasting intensifies your ability to concentrate. Fasting for the day is about realizing that food is a pleasure and that Yom Kippur is not a day of pleasure. It's a day of contemplation.

Once you get over the first hour or two, I find that it doesn't really matter that I'm fasting, and I don't miss the food. But I will tell you that probably an hour before the end of ne'ilah, *which is the last part of the Yom Kippur service, I'm starving.*

After Yom Kippur there is a break-the-fast buffet at our synagogue. Community is at the heart of Judaism. Our congregation is a community with a commitment to Jewish integrity. Our Rabbi, Elyse Frishman, speaks often about living Jewishly, which roughly translates, for me, to observing and living as close to Reform Jewish tradition as possible.

If you would ask me to describe Judaism, it's ethical monotheism, with a heavy dose of community. We're a people. It is all about family and community.

Richard D. Cameron is a businessman, a fifty-four-year-old "baby boomer," who has been married for thirty-one years. He and his wife have two daughters.

exploring a great spiritual practice

chaptereight

The Season of Lent

When Christians today observe the penitential season of Lent, they mean the forty days between Ash Wednesday and Easter, which usually fall somewhere during the months of March and April. The word "Lent" comes from the Anglo-Saxon *lencten*, meaning spring. (For word buffs, Lent and length have the same root; in spring the days lengthen.)

While the self-affliction of Yom Kippur is rooted in the Hebrew Scriptures and Ramadan fasting is prescribed in the *Qu'ran*, no such origin for Lenten fasting exists in the Christian Scriptures. As we saw in chapter 3, the Lenten season itself does not appear until the early centuries of Christianity.

Many Christians today believe that Lent is modeled on Jesus' forty-day fast in the desert. The symbolic connection is valid and important, but it seems likely that the relationship was emphasized only after a much shorter pre-Easter fast was expanded and Lent as a liturgical season was well established. In the early days of the church, another forty-day fast—after the Epiphany, which celebrates Jesus' baptism—was traditional for many Christians. This fast was the one held to be in imitation of Jesus' desert experience, which, the Gospels say, took place after his baptism in the Jordan. The importance of the model was never in doubt. As the Epiphany fast declined and the Lenten season became universal, the symbolic connection migrated to match the liturgical calendar.

The Basics

In each of the three Christian paths that we followed in chapter 4—Roman Catholicism, Eastern Orthodoxy, and Protestantism—the contemporary experience of Lent is different. We will look briefly at the basic practices in each tradition before moving onto the spiritual dimensions of Lenten fasting.

Roman Catholic Tradition. Catholics who remember observing Lent in the first half of the twentieth century remember it as a time of strict rules for fast and abstinence but also a time for exceptions and dispensations. In 1966, the rules changed as Pope Paul VI undertook to explain that the times required modifications in the overly legalistic code facing contemporary Catholics. He recommended that local churches adapt the regulations on fast and abstinence to their populations.

Today in the United States there are only two obligatory days of fasting for Roman Catholics—Ash Wednesday and Good Friday. The Fridays of Lent are days of abstinence, meaning that those observing the practice may not eat meat. Although pastoral teaching since 1966 has urged voluntary fasting during Lent and voluntary abstinence on the other Fridays of the year, most Catholics heard only the suspension of rules, not the substitution of voluntary Lenten practices. And while Catholic preaching may occasionally note the importance of fasting during Lent, the practice is more frequently ignored or overlooked. As one Catholic educator says, "In our time, there is a peculiar ambivalence about fasting."

Eastern Orthodox Churches. To western observers, the most obvious difference about the Orthodox season of Lent is the date it ends. Because Orthodox churches still follow the Julian calendar instead of the Gregorian calendar, Easter (*Pascha*) can fall anywhere from one to six weeks after the western celebration of Easter. (In some years, the dates do coincide.) But there are also differences in the beginning of Lenten observances—and in the rules for fasting.

Orthodox teaching prescribes the pre-Lenten weeks as spiritual preparation for Great Lent. Two weeks before Lent, on Meatfare Sunday, the faithful are expected to stop eating meat, fish and poultry and not resume until *Pascha*. The last Sunday before Lent is called Cheesefare Sunday because that is the last day for eating dairy products. In most eastern churches, Lent begins the next day—on a Monday, not a Wednesday as in western churches. Thus, the Orthodox fast for seven full weeks—somewhat longer than the forty days of western tradition—and during that time they do not eat meat, fish, oil, dairy products or drink alcoholic beverages.

While there are some variations in fasting rules among the Orthodox churches and all the churches note a distinct lack of interest among their faithful, fasting during Holy and Great Lent, as the season is called in the eastern tradition, remains a rigorous discipline. It is seen as a positive discipline, however, as a healthy way of strengthening the soul, not punishing the body.

Protestant Churches. Fasting during Lent is, by and large, not a spiritual practice for most Protestants.

In mainline churches where Lent is an acceptable season there are no longer any fasting rules to be followed. In the Anglican Church, for example, *The Book of Common Prayer* suggests "special acts of discipline and self-denial" for Lent, but the practice is left to the discretion of the individual. Other Protestant Christians, if they choose to fast at all, limit the practice, as Roman Catholics do, to Ash Wednesday and Good Friday.

In the evangelical or free churches, liturgical seasons like Lent are not generally observed.

Other Protestant Christians, if they choose to fast at all, limit the practice, as Roman Catholics do, to Ash Wednesday and Good Friday.

Alternative Interpretations

The case for fasting from something other than food is stated well by a Catholic woman religious:

> *Personally, I find fasting awkward. I have spent my life on diets. At the present time, a day of fast is little different from an ordinary day for me, because I try mightily to limit the food I eat. So I have been trying to*

invest new meaning in fasting. I think fasting should be accompanied by a conscious donation of money to help feed the poor of the world. Fasting should be seen as an act of solidarity with the poor of the world—we can choose to fast; they cannot. I am also seeing that there are a variety of forms of fasting: from too much TV, from entertainment, from consumerism—whatever can keep us from growing in relation to God and others and our environment. So fasting is valuable now as in the past, but only if it helps to free us from enslavement to whatever keeps us from harmony with God, community, and nature.

She distills for us some central elements of Christian fasting: deepening our relationship with God, with others, especially the poor, and with nature. And she has captured the dilemma of many contemporary Christians who do not find fasting from food a meaningful way to achieve such spiritual objectives. Those Christians are increasingly comfortable with alternative kinds of fasting.

◆ The choices for such practices are unlimited. One can fast from any unhealthy trait—gossip, lethargy, or discontent— and aim for its opposite—silence, enthusiasm, or gratitude. It is important, practitioners say, to select the appropriate fast or feast and persevere through the Lenten season.

◆ Other Christians, struggling in the midst of a consumer-happy society, choose to focus their Lenten fasting on living more simply. For forty days, they try to limit their purchases of unnecessary items—clothes, jewelry, gadgets, or whatever inhibits them from responding to God. This kind of fasting, they say, is not just personal reform, which they may hope will last beyond Easter. It also draws their attention to the planet's limited resources and to the needs of the poor.

◆ The seasons of Lent and Easter are not only liturgical seasons with specific dates on the calendar. Christians often interpret them as symbolic seasons in life. And fasting can be a spiritually significant part of such times. A young man who took a three-week service trip to a developing-world country said:

I wanted to travel light—without the encumbrances of things I consider necessities and are really luxuries. So my preparation resembled Lent—giving up and doing without. And yes, the trip was a difficult lesson in how people live with less—less food, less comfort, less control over their environment. But what I did not expect is that the trip itself, instead of being a continuation of Lent, became Easter—filled with wonderful signs of God's presence.

Spiritual Dimensions

For Christians, Lenten practices offer a variety of spiritual messages. Prayer and almsgiving, as Lenten disciplines, are rather well understood. Fasting is not. There is clearly a contemporary emphasis on proper motivation—an effort to move beyond the negative inheritance focused on guilt and sin and the idea of the body as evil. "Penance," the Jesuit priest Robert Taft has written, "does not turn people into Christians." And Rev. Carol Peterson, a Lutheran pastor, says that while she would not discourage someone in her community from fasting, "I would want to be sure there is no pathology there."

The significant task for Christians is to focus on the spiritual dimensions of fasting, whatever form the practice takes, and transform what could be solely a negative act into a freeing experience of spiritual growth.

One way to understand this Christian effort is to draw on the idea of conversion (*metanoia*), which is a biblical concept meaning a change of mind or heart. Martin Luther understood *metanoia* as "coming to one's senses." Lenten fasting is a way to strip away unessential elements of life in order to see more clearly the important things. *Metanoia* requires a turning away and a turning toward. Let's look at three aspects of this Lenten conversion experience.

Penance does not turn people into Christians.

Robert Taft

- ◆ Turning away from self. Christian teaching speaks of this effort as "dying to self that we may rise again in Christ." This is not self-discipline for its own sake, but a turning away from self-absorbed actions to achieve the freedom to focus on a deeper life. Lent, Joan Chittister writes, is "the time to make new efforts to be what we say we want to be." Fasting, in the Christian context, provides an opportunity to refocus everyday priorities and awaken to the presence of God.

- ◆ Turning toward God. Christians who have fasted during Lent say the experience has left them with a distinct awareness of their need for God and of their own vulnerability. Sometimes they are "successful"—completing forty days of the discipline they have chosen. At other times, they "fail"—unable to be faithful to what they promised. Fasting is an experience of human limitations and *metanoia* can happen even in times of "failure."

◆ Turning toward others. As Roman Catholics have moved away from general Lenten fasting, they have lost what the Orthodox churches are struggling to keep alive—the corporate nature of fasting. A community fasts together, supporting one another in the effort. (As we have seen, this sense of community-wide fasting also appears in Judaism on Yom Kippur and in Islam during Ramadan.) The priest David Buersmeyer suggests the Catholic community should "move away from promoting Lent primarily on the grounds of personal spiritual benefits" and "move toward emphasizing our shared time, our shared story, our bonding as a pilgrim people who hunger for God."

The other sense in which fasting fosters a turning toward others is in its connection to the poor. From its biblical roots, when Isaiah spoke to the Jewish people, and continuing through two centuries of teaching, Christian fasting embraces not only a deeper solidarity with those who are hungry or suffering but also an effort to alleviate some of their misery. Charity mingles with social justice.

Contemporary teaching also suggests that the practice of fasting confront and attempt to relieve the strain on our planet's natural resources.

The effort to turn toward others is the bottom line. Any spiritual practice, Christians believe, must lead outward. Lenten fasting is no exception.

Joan Marie Clark

My Lenten fasting was pretty nonexistent until about six or seven years ago when I seem to have been led to fast—to eat and drink nothing but water—for one day a week during Lent. I say "led" because this wasn't something someone told me to do or I read about in a book or I decided on my own. The inspiration came from somewhere deep inside me and I had to respond. Now I'm grateful I did, but at that time it wasn't all that clear and it certainly wasn't easy.

That first Lent I selected a day, usually Wednesdays, and I would not eat after dinner on Tuesday evening until breakfast on Thursday. The simplicity of the effort cleared my head— no exceptions to deal with, just a regular weekly fast with a beginning and an end.

I came to see each weekly fast as a three-day "desert experience." The day before the fast, I became aware of every time I was hungry and could eat. I knew I could choose to eat that day and I began to feel, really feel, a sense of what the poor of the world go through. They have no choice. I dreaded the fast day coming up and each week I struggled with my fears that I wouldn't make it through. I was tempted to gorge at dinner to tide myself through. The fast day itself, as difficult as it was, became a truly spiritual day, a retreat day really. There was more time to pray and my prayer was so much deeper and less self-centered. I felt what I prayed. There was time to read from Scripture and I began to understand what it means to hunger after the word of God. Those days each passage I read took on new meaning. The third day, when I ate again, I was filled with gratitude. Even a banana looked beautiful. Gradually I began to direct this gratitude to God for leading me to fast.

Then came what I called the "in between days." I guess I had thought I would be able to forget about fasting until the next week. But as Lent wore on, and I saw that the fast days weren't getting any easier physically— although I didn't get headaches, I still felt the hunger pangs—these middle days became spiritual, too. I don't like to think of myself as having cravings or addictions or dependencies. But I was amazed to find how much time I spent planning when and where and what to eat. I felt my reliance on God more deeply and I understood my own weaknesses more clearly. I saw my impatience, my need to control, my lack of faith and trust in God, my lack of sympathy for others. And each week I was thrown back on God's help to get me through.

I did discuss all this with my spiritual director. She was concerned at first, I think, wondering if I were mired in some old-fashioned negative practice, but when I described for her how present God was in the experience and how I felt more connected to others and more committed to my work and more responsive at Sunday liturgies, she talked about "fruits," about recognizing those actions that truly come from the Spirit by the presence of new or deeper virtues in your life. When we looked back during Holy Week she said that fasting for me had been an experience of grace. I can look back now and even read some of the entries in my journal and see that she was right.

I have fasted that way most years since then. Some Lents have been a little easier and some just as hard. I know fasting is not a popular Lenten practice these days. But for me it has been a profound spiritual experience that has changed my life. It allowed my relationship with God to deepen and that's what Lent is all about.

Joan Marie Clarke, who is a Catholic, lives in Baltimore. She is single, cares for an elderly mother, and practices as a family therapist. She prefers this pseudonym.

Voices

Louise Theiller

I grew up in a Catholic family and my mother was always very religious. Every Lent we had to give up something and Catholic schools reinforced that. [As we grew older] we only ate one full meal a day. What's so amazing is that I still do what I did at seven and at fourteen. Giving up the candy and not eating in between meals, those were the main things we did during Lent. I still do that. That sounds terrible, doesn't it? That I still do as an adult what I did as a child? I should do more as an adult, but what you do as a child seems to carry over into your adult years.

I look forward to Lent because it's an opportunity to change my eating habits. It's a healthier life style during Lent. Lent has always been a time of penance, forever. I was always taught that. So if I don't do that, Easter won't have the same significance.

It took me a while to change [after the rules changed in the 60s] but now I realize the reasons for it. You should do something more, rather than just giving up something. I don't think what we did was bad because it made you feel different and special. But maybe they changed things and we weren't ready to listen to what we should put in place of what we were doing.

My children are actively Catholic. Fasting to them means giving up something during Lent. That's what I did with them when they were growing up. My daughter passed away. My two grandchildren are being raised by my son-in-law and his new wife. And they fast. During Lent they give up something like wine or beer or whatever. And they make a point of telling the children that the children also have to give up something. I'm very impressed with that. My two granddaughters give up candy or ice cream. They like to say that they're doing something special.

People don't think what I do is fasting. Well, we always called it fasting. It's what I was taught. What amazes me is that in our parish it's never preached about. The rules are always in our weekly bulletin, but no one ever teaches us about fasting. I've never been exposed to the idea that fasting focuses you to pray and makes your spiritual life stronger. Even in school I don't *remember that being emphasized. Maybe they think we can get that message from the story of Jesus going into the desert to pray, but I don't remember it being stressed. Learning more about fasting may help us as Christians get back to praying more.*

I will try to keep up fasting even though I'm over sixty. That's because my mother did and she's always been a positive influence on me. I wouldn't feel right if it were Lent and I didn't do something.

Louise Theiller was educated in Catholic schools for fourteen years, has been married for forty-three years, and is a mother and grandmother.

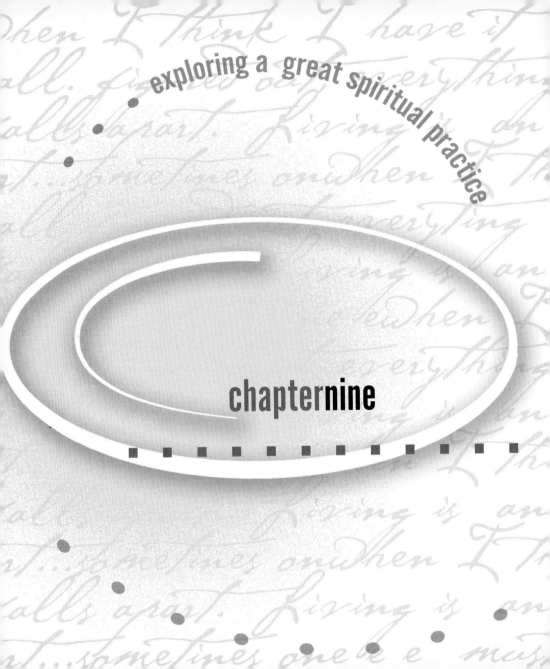

exploring a great spiritual practice

chapter**nine**

Ramadan
Fasting

There are an estimated seven million Muslims in the United States. They come from a variety of ethnic backgrounds and from many countries; they are African Americans and Arab Americans, born in cities, suburbs, and rural areas of the United States, as well as recent immigrants. Fasting during Ramadan binds them together in observing one of the most basic duties of their faith.

Imam Mohammad Quatanani, who came to the United States from Jordan in 1996, serves as Imam at a large suburban mosque where the community numbers more than one thousand Muslim men and women. It is easy to speak to all of them, he says, no matter what their national origin or their language. "The *Qur'an* joins us."

Still, those who have visited a predominantly Arabic country during Ramadan notice interesting differences. In Arabic countries, Ramadan fasting affects the society as a whole. One business traveler to Egypt says he cannot do business there during Ramadan. "Everything stops," he says. "People are taking naps. They don't show up for appointments. They're cranky because they're not smoking. Nothing gets done for a month." In the United States, Muslims, like Christians or Jews or Hindus, blend into the culture and are expected to function normally at jobs and in school, no matter what their religious obligations require.

The Basics

he Calendar. Unlike Yom Kippur and Lent, observances that may vary slightly from one year to the next but remain rooted in certain months, Ramadan, the ninth month of the Islamic calendar, is a totally movable season. Each year it begins about eleven days earlier, moving in the western calendar from January, to December, November, October, on into the long days of the summer months, and back to January.

For Muslims, the Ramadan fast starts before sunrise—traditionally, when it is just light enough to see the difference between a black and a white thread—and continues until it is so dark that the same threads are indistinguishable. Practically, most mosques issue precise printed schedules, showing local Muslims the times for fasting for each day of Ramadan. During the summer months, when daylight can stretch for twelve or more hours and the heat can be oppressive, Ramadan fasting is indeed rigorous.

Late in the month of Ramadan there is one special occasion called *Lailat ul-Qadr* (or the Night of Power), which commemorates the time the *Qur'an* was first revealed to Mohammad. The rules of fasting do not change for *Lailat ul-Qadr*, but, in addition, many Muslims spend that night in prayer at the mosque.

The Fast and the meals that surround it. The rules of Islam are strict: nothing may pass your lips once the fast has begun. That means that Muslims don't eat anything, drink anything (including water), smoke, brush their teeth, or take medication during the daylight hours of Ramadan. Muslims must also abstain from any sexual activity during the time of fasting.

Bracketing each day's fast are two meals:

◆ Each evening, Muslims break their fast with a meal called *Iftar*. Some Muslims will first break their fast with dates, a food the Prophet Mohammad enjoyed, and a glass of water, then pause to say evening prayers, and finally have a celebratory dinner. Like Jews on Yom Kippur, Muslims do not like to break their fast alone. Families, neighbors, and friends may gather for *Iftar* and many Muslims will go to a mosque to break the fast. Ramadan teaching includes caring for the poor. In some places the hungry from the neighborhood may be invited to the mosque for *Iftar*; in others, the Muslim community may bring food to them.

◆ Each night's meal is a celebratory time, the end of a time of fasting, but also a time for fellowship and good food. Many Muslim women say they actually gain weight during Ramadan; despite the rigors of the daytime fast, Ramadan is not, they say, a time to diet.

◆ The Prophet, who did not believe fasting should be an overwhelming hardship, also recommended a meal before each day's fast begins. And Islamic tradition recommends that this meal, *Sahoor,* should be taken as close to sunrise as possible. Muslims say that eating *Sahoor* is not an obligation but a blessing. Depending on the time of year, some rise very early, eat or take a glass of water and return to bed until the alarm rings again for their regular daytime routine.

Celebrating the end of the fast. Ramadan ends, as it began, at the sighting of a new moon, which signals the beginning of the next month, Shawwal. The first day of Shawwal, called *Eid al-Fitr*, which can be translated as Feast of the Fast-Breaking, is one of the two major celebrations in the Islamic calendar. Muslims view *Eid al-Fitr* as a time of joy and thanksgiving; it is the end of a month of fasting, marking the completion of a demanding discipline, but it is not a feast for gluttony or frivolity. Rather, Muslims say, it is a spiritual time, with an emphasis on gratitude for one's blessings and on forgiveness and kindness toward others.

So Muslims begin three days of festivities with prayer. Like the many Christians who fill churches for Easter services, large numbers of Muslims, who may not normally pray together at their mosque, gather for *Eid al-Fitr*. The celebration takes place shortly after sunrise and, to accommodate the crowds, it is often held outdoors in an arena or park or in a large mosque. After they pray, Muslims break their month-long Ramadan fast with family and friends.

Muslims say it is a **spiritual** time, with an emphasis on **gratitude** for one's **blessings** and on **forgiveness** and **kindness** toward **others.**

An essential part of *Eid al-Fitr* is a donation to charity, which all Muslims must make before the end of Ramadan. Called *Zakat al-Fitr*, this donation was traditionally a gift of food to someone who was hungry, but nowadays it can be given as a cash donation to one's mosque or to a Muslim charitable organization and directed toward feeding the poor.

Muslims view *Zakat al*-Fitr—a special form of *zakat*, which is one of the Five Pillars of Islam—not only as an obligation but also as a privilege, a way of thanking Allah for their own blessings.

Spiritual Dimensions

The rhythm of Ramadan fasting is unmistakable. Each day contains both fasting and feasting and each day of the month Muslims must begin the cycle again. The steady repetition of arduous fast with intermittent feasting provides valuable spiritual insights. Muslims say that Ramadan deepens their bonds with each other and their awareness of the poor. Knowing that millions of people around the world are fasting together sends an eloquent message to all participants. Being hungry day after day offers a visceral way to understand the powerlessness of the poor. The celebration of *Iftar* each evening brings recurrent messages of joy and thanksgiving.

Islamic scholar Cyril Glasse illuminates two further lessons. Ramadan provides:

◆ An experience of limitation. The season imposes a clear limit to indulgence day after day for a month. The limitation on our freedom gives us knowledge, he says; through the experience we come to know ourselves as we are. "Without limitation, knowledge is impossible, for it is when we come to the end or limit of a thing that its true nature becomes evident."

◆ An experience of purification. Glasse compares fasting to "the pruning of trees." Removing dead branches makes for stronger trees and learning to curb one's appetites makes for stronger human beings. In Islam, Ramadan fasting is the spiritual discipline that works toward that goal.

Nevine

I grew up in Alexandria, Egypt, and it is always very pleasant to be back home during the holy month of Ramadan. There is a feeling of community and compassion. Sixty million people all fasting from sunrise to sunset. Nobody would think of having a meal in public, even the non-Muslims. After sunset, the streets are deserted for about forty-five minutes, while everybody is eating. If you walk in the streets of any major city in Egypt, the only sound would be the banging of cutlery. It is very special. Maybe that encourages one to fast, that sense of solidarity.

Most people do not break their fast alone. One is constantly invited somewhere for Iftar, the meal at sunset. In Egypt my cousins would come over one day or we would go to them. We would often go to my mother or my mother-in-law. It is a month where families see more of each other.

People who have to be in the streets, for example policemen, doormen, taxi chauffeurs, doctors on call, etc., can break their fast in the streets on the food provided by well-off families or people who cannot fast. A lot of buildings and mosques place tables on the sidewalks and cover them with food for whoever needs it.

There are some differences depending on the country. In Egypt we all eat our main meal when the sun sets. In Morocco, where we also lived for a few years, people break their fast alone at home, usually on soup and desserts, and then they go out in the streets for a walk. The streets are so crowded with people of all ages, even several main avenues become only for pedestrians. They then start visiting each other and drink tea and then have their main meal at around 8 or 9 pm.

Now here in the States, I sometimes do it the Moroccan way. I have a cup of tea, a sandwich and something sweet at sunset, then my main meal at around 8 or 9 pm and I go to bed at my usual time, without waking up or staying up late at night to eat again before sunrise. Some people in Egypt entertain for Sahoor, the meal before the first rays of the sun appear.

When one is fasting one cannot put anything in your mouth, no food, no drink, and one has to abstain from any sexual relations. I take my vitamins, calcium, and statins when I break my fast. Not everybody fasts easily. I have a cousin who really feels bad the first few days. Some people get headaches or cannot concentrate. Some cannot sleep and others need more sleep. Luckily, I fast easily, but I sort of lose my energy a few hours before sunset.

Of course the fast is much harder, it is terrible, when it comes during the summer months. Every year it comes about eleven days in advance [earlier than the previous year]. I remember we were living in Washington about twenty years ago and Ramadan was in summer then. Sunset was after 8 pm. The worst part was not drinking anything in the heat and humidity.

Ramadan is not just about abstaining from food and drink. It is a whole different way of living. One should be polite, good-natured, and pleasant. Living in New York City can be very time consuming. One can forget about so many things. Then during Ramadan, one restores one's faith. One starts to think about religion and faith and read the Qur'an and it is a step in the right direction. Ramadan is a month when I try to change my life as much as possible and become a better Muslim.

Nevine is a graphic designer; her husband is a diplomat. They have lived in France, Yugoslavia, Morocco, New York, and are now in Washington, D.C. She chooses to use only her first name.

Voices

Mary Aktay

My husband is Muslim and I'm Catholic. When we were first married, almost thirty years ago now, my husband's relatives would say things like, "Oh, Americans could never fast." Being the Peter Rabbit person that I am, anything I'm told I can't do, that's exactly what I'm going to do. So I said, "Okay, fine." I didn't fast right away because I got pregnant and pregnant and nursing women are exempt from fasting. So it wasn't until the girls were maybe six and three that I started in earnest.

Basically, I fasted in solidarity with my husband. Our girls were baptized, they received Communion, they were confirmed. So they have been raised Christian. [Fasting] is one thing I do to say, "You know what? We are a Christian family, but we are also a Muslim family."

During Ramadan, sometimes, not very often, but sometimes, we have gone to the mosque to break the fast. My husband would go to prayers, and I would be downstairs in the kitchen helping the women and then serving Iftar. Everybody's invited, Muslim and non-Muslim. The doors are open, and when we were there, a lot of people, who, well, if they weren't homeless they were pretty close to it, would come in and have a hot meal and be very grateful for it.

Yes, fasting is difficult, especially in the beginning. They say you fast from dawn, which is not really sunrise, it's maybe two or three hours before sunrise, to maybe an hour after sunset. It has to be so dark that you cannot distinguish a white thread from a black thread. That's when you can break the fast. When it's light enough to see the difference between the threads, you're supposed to be fasting.

The first two days, as your body adjusts, you do get the very bad headaches. I know some people who prepare themselves for it for a few weeks prior to Ramadan. They will fast one or two days of the week to gradually introduce it. My problem is more of stopping myself from patting myself on the back. People used to say, "Oh, Mary, how do you do that?" with such admiration. That's not why you're supposed to be fasting, to get the admiration of other people. And I would go out of my way to say, "No, it's really not that bad."

And it isn't. I've been doing the Ramadan fast for about twenty years. I continue to do it because it gives me time to think what it must be like for people who don't have the luxury of eating at six o'clock or whenever. I know I'm going to be eating and eating rather well, given my middle-class American lifestyle. But for those eight, ten, twelve hours, whatever it is during the day that I'm not eating or drinking, it makes me very mindful about what 70 percent of this world goes through.

The rationale in Ramadan is that it's not about giving up food. It's about not doing anything else during the day that would take your mind off God. At first I wondered how that could be since when you're hungry all you can think of is food. Then, as I got older and wiser, I started thinking, well, where does the food come from? The food comes from the grace of God. And then that brought me into justice issues and solidarity with the poor. The food comes from the grace of God, but it also comes from the sweat and the labor of people like the migrant farm workers.

The other thing about my Ramadan fasting is that I feel in solidarity with Muslim brothers and sisters. I think that, especially post-9/11, we should look for what we share together. The ethical underpinnings of the religions are the same. There is a concern for the poor. There is a concern for more equitable distribution of the wealth and sharing. I would say Ramadan fasting has made me a better Christian.

Mary Aktay, a writer, and her husband, Servet, who was raised in Turkey, raised their two daughters in suburban New Jersey.

exploring a great spiritual practice

chapterten

PoliticalFasting: SendingaMessage andMakingConnections

Judaism, Christianity, and Islam all connect their seasons of fasting to messages of care and concern for others—the poor, the hungry, the oppressed. But adherents of these religions are not the only ones who fast to express their compassion or their commitment to a cause. Nonviolent political actions aimed at changing oppressive structures have long included fasting and have long included Hindus, Buddhists, atheists, humanists, and many others who simply describe themselves as "not religious."

Throughout the twentieth century, some of these marches, vigils, demonstrations, and political acts have indeed been dramatic examples of devotion to a cause. The century began with hunger strikes by English suffragettes and by a spokesman for Irish independence, Terence MacSwiney. In Mid-century, Mahatma Gandhi made fasting a part of the nonviolent political actions that achieved India's independence from British rule, and in Rome, Dorothy Day and nineteen other women fasted for ten days during the Second Vatican Council, advocating a peace statement that supported both conscientious objection and a ban on nuclear weapons. In more recent years, fasting has been part of the peace movement in its struggles against nuclear armament, oppression in Latin America, and war in Iraq.

We can also trace a connection between many famine crises around the world and specific days of fasting that brought increased contributions to alleviate the hunger and greater public awareness of the situation. Fast days proclaimed for Ethiopia, Poland, and Guatemala, to name just three examples, joined people of many religions with those of no religious affiliation to a common cause.

In this chapter we will consider the role fasting plays in two kinds of response to hunger, war, and political oppression. First, we will look at fasting among a relatively small but vocal and committed group—the people who participate in contemporary political actions for peace and justice. Second, we will look at what fasting means for a broader group, often young people, who express their solidarity with the hungry by participating in fasting events sponsored by nonprofit organizations such as Oxfam, Catholic Relief Services, and World Vision.

Fasting for Peace and Justice

Fasting has deep roots in both the American civil rights movement and the peace movement. Charismatic leaders like Martin Luther King, Cesar Chavez, and Daniel and Philip Berrigan all recognized the power of fasting. How can we understand the connection between fasting and political action?

Participants note that political actions, like marches, demonstrations, or vigils, allow them to make a statement, express their indignation, provide a voice for the powerless, become part of something larger than their own self-interest.

Advocates say that being hungry, whether it's for only one day or for a longer forty-day fast, enhances their understanding of hunger and thirst, not only for food and water but also for peace and justice.

The act of fasting adds an extra dimension to their commitment. It says they are willing to subject themselves to discomfort to give weight to their convictions and to express their solidarity with other human beings who are suffering. It is for many participants a necessary ethical response to an alarming situation.

In this context, we look more closely at two aspects of fasting.

First, fasting is part of the personal preparation for the action; it is a way to "clear the decks"—to clarify intent and focus one's attention. Advocates say that being hungry, whether it's for only one day or for a longer forty-day fast, enhances their understanding of hunger and thirst, not only for food and water but also for peace and justice.

The Jesuit priest G. Simon Harak, who has fasted as part of the peace movement for more than twenty years (see *Voices*, page 114), says that participants must first clear away any negative motivations that surround fasting. Giving up food, which is essentially a negative act, should not be used to express self-destructive patterns in an individual. Nor should fasting express a desire to punish the society. One cannot, he says, go into a political fast thinking, for example, "When I hurt myself, then they'll have to pay attention."

We see here a clear expression of what peace activists say is the bottom-line difference between a hunger strike and a political fast: A hunger strike does violence to the participant and attempts to hold others hostage to a particular agenda, which is also a violent act.

Rather, Harak says, fasting as a political act stems from our recognition of the dignity of every individual, our own and those for whom we fast. Fasting is a supremely human act. Animals can't fast. They can go without food, but they can't choose to fast. Once we are in contact with our own self-worth, Father Harak concludes, fasting becomes a positive act, which allows us to express our human freedom and our personal values.

Rose Marie Berger, a member of Sojourners, an ecumenical Christian community based in Washington, D.C., has also fasted frequently for peace. She believes that fasting always has a political aspect. Fasting is a way of "unhooking ourselves from a consumer culture, realigning ourselves with our deeper selves, and being open to whatever happens." She explains with her own experience: "I live in a culture where all kinds of things are preying on my soul. For me the tradition of fasting, and making it a regular component of my spiritual life, helps me remember that I'm not beholden to all these things that want to lay claim to me, that I'm spiritually free and that I can act out of that spiritual freedom."

Members of the peace movement, she says, choose to fast to open themselves up to creative possibilities—what they hope will be new ways to solve intractable problems.

Second, fasting can also be viewed as an essential element of the action itself. For observers and participants alike, fasting makes a clear connection between personal behavior and political responsibility. It demonstrates individual commitment and it is a way to draw attention to the cause.

Father Harak says: "You can't think of yourself except as a member of a community. To be isolated is really an inconceivable thought. . . . Once we see the human as an essentially social being, then physical statements of every kind, from parades and juggling to fasting and demonstrations, have an impact on the society's self-understanding. So when we fast in solidarity, we, in a sense, use our hunger as an engine for the desire for peace and justice for a particular group of people, whoever they may be. We are bringing the hunger of those for whom we fast into the body politic and we are calling for the body politic to respond."

Highlighting a somewhat different example, Ms. Berger notes that in the Middle East, "there have been a number of times when groups have come together across the lines of division—Palestinians and Israelis, Christians and Jews and Orthodox—simply saying to each other, 'We don't know what else to do because our cultures are at war, but we will fast together and pray together through silence.'" The fasting and the silence, she says, "changed something in those people. In the openness that fasting allowed, they developed respect for each other. They were then able to go back to their communities and serve to some small extent as peacemakers, as people who brought a different perspective."

There are, she says, illustrations of dramatic public statements like Sister Diana Ortiz' 1996 Fast for Truth in front of the White House and at other times "small hidden examples of how people try to practice the discipline of fasting in a way that leads to more peaceful co-existence." Both are valid expressions of commitment.

Fasting to Alleviate Hunger

The statistics are startling: more than eight hundred thousand people in the world are hungry and more than one hundred fifty thousand of them are children under five. When confronted with facts like these, many Americans have responded by participating in a fast event. Their motives are usually threefold: To deepen their own awareness of global hunger; to raise funds to alleviate even a small part of the problem; and to draw the attention of others to the situation.

To understand this aspect of political fasting we consider three nonprofit organizations and their fast events.

◆ In 1974, Oxfam America, a member of Oxfam International which is dedicated to finding long-term solutions to global poverty and hunger, initiated its "Fast for a World Harvest" campaign. That year more than two hundred and fifty thousand people fasted on the Thursday before Thanksgiving and donated the money they saved to Oxfam.

While Nathan Gray, the founder of the Fast, saw a connection between fasting and the harvest, Fast events are no longer confined to one Thursday in November. And there is great variety in the kinds of "fasts" people undertake. On some college campuses there are dining hall fasts where students skip one meal and a donation goes to Oxfam. Many events do not involve fasting at all; community groups arrange concerts, talent shows, and auctions to raise money and awareness.

◆ Catholic Relief Services (CRS), sponsors of "Operation Rice Bowl," which collects donations for the poor from

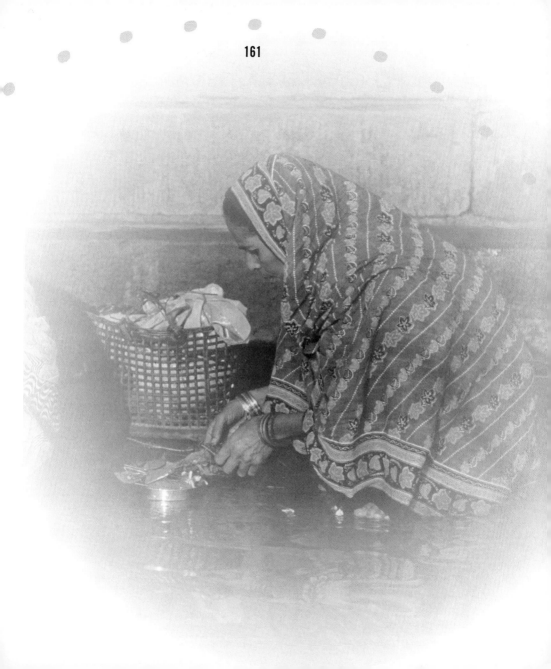

Catholics during Lent, also offers "Food Fast," a twenty-four-hour hunger awareness retreat for high-school students. The agency estimates that between thirty-five thousand and forty thousand students participate in a "Food Fast" each year. CRS encourages youth groups to experience the retreat as time to learn about the realities of hunger and to make a commitment to participate in alleviating the problem.

◆ World Vision, a Christian relief organization, sponsors a youth program called "The 30-Hour Famine." Although events can be held at any time, the organization names annual National Famine Dates and suggests that youth

groups raise money from sponsors and donors and then fast for thirty hours. The funds go to World Vision to be used in relieving global hunger. In 2002, more than six hundred thousand students participated in "The 30-Hour Famine."

All three organizations are aware that this is an age of epidemic eating disorders. Their fasts are short in duration and will probably cause no physical harm, they say, but when young people are encouraged to participate in such fast events, wisdom indicates that they be supervised and that individuals at risk be offered alternatives to fasting from food.

Voices

G. Simon Harak, S.J.

I had been in the Society of Jesus for a couple of years. I had heard that people fasted, that Jesus fasted and saints fasted so I thought I ought to try it. But I never could. I finally said to my spiritual director, "I try to fast, but I can't." He said, "That's because you're fasting for yourself. Fast for someone else, then you'll be able to fast."

Well, then I had a close friend who had kidney stones so I said to myself, "I'll fast that God will take care of his kidney stones, through the hospital, doctors, whatever." How did I undertake this fast? I was going to skip dessert for just one meal. But I lived in a community where we had a cook who made lemon meringue pie, which is without reservation my favorite dessert of all time. So I'm standing there at the end of food line and looking at the lemon meringue pie and thinking, "Surely God doesn't want me to give up lemon meringue pie. I could fast tomorrow." I'm going through all this rationalization trying to find a way I could get this lemon meringue pie.

And all of a sudden, I stepped back and looked at myself and I thought, "Simon, you think you're so spiritual and you're losing the battle to a piece of lemon meringue pie. What's going on?" So I started to laugh at myself and it was then that I could fast. That moment of laughter let me see that fasting is a special gift, that I can't do this myself. I can't even hold out against a piece of lemon meringue pie. It was partly my love for my friend and mostly God's love for me that enabled me to shake my head and walk away. You have to love someone else and you have to realize God loves you; otherwise you're not going to be able to skip even a piece of lemon meringue pie, let alone fast for 10 or 20 or 40 days.

[The next step] I guess was fasting for the day on Good Friday. I was trying to reach a deeper communion with Jesus and so I undertook to fast that day. Then I began to fast on Tuesdays for my students and the university community. Then sometime in the 80s the Catholic bishops suggested a Friday fast for peace. So I did that, too. But by then, I had a lot of Jewish and Muslim friends and I saw that they don't wimp fast the way we Catholics do. So I had changed to fasting the way they do—no food or liquid for the day.

When I started to fast for the people of Iraq, I came with what I already had, my religious or prayer commitment. That's what I brought to the political fast. But I have to tell you *that every single time I fast, I have to start all over and ask myself, "What am I doing this for?" I have to look at my willingness to punish myself or to punish other people into listening to me. And if I do find those kinds of self-destructive tendencies or if I see that I'm becoming short-tempered or condescending, I stop the fast immediately. At that moment I'm in the kitchen eating. Continuing my fast under those conditions would be destructive and not what God wants.*

For me, the personal, the political, the spiritual—they aren't divided into mutually exclusive categories. I know that God wants justice and so for me to fast is to align myself with God in God's own hunger and thirst for justice. Not everybody thinks this way, but I think this way. I am active in two peace organizations. "Voices in the Wilderness" is a relatively new group and it's not religiously based, just people from all over who don't want to see people suffer and die. The War Resisters League is the oldest nonviolent organization in the United States, but they also are resolutely secular. So while fasting for me also has a religious dimension, that isn't necessarily there for the other people who are fasting for the same political reasons. And I understand that.

When I'm talking to people who may be fasting for the first time or who want to start a political fast, I love to tell the story of myself and the lemon meringue pie. It's a good place to start because everybody thinks, "Oh gosh, this guy, he couldn't even give up a lemon meringue pie at first and now he's fasting for days. I've got a shot." And that's a good thing.

G. Simon Harak, S.J., is a Jesuit priest living in New York City. He is the author of *Virtuous Passions: The Formation of Christian Character* and editor of *Nonviolence for the Third Millennium: Its Legacy and Its Future* and serves as Anti-Militarism Coordinator of the War Resisters League.

Stephen Land

In 1974, while I was still in college, someone at a card table by the science center had materials about Oxfam and their first Fast for a World Harvest. I found Oxfam's support for the neediest appealing, so I wanted to do something for them. The idea behind the Fast was that anybody could afford it—even a student—because you give up eating for the day and what you would spend on food you give away. As appealing as that was, I didn't really like the idea of not eating for a day. So I gave some money, but I didn't fast.

And, of course, I got on their mailing list. I kept giving money and eventually they asked me to join the Board. But I didn't fast for quite awhile. In the early 80s I organized a fast at my church during the Lenten season and we gave the money to Oxfam. I was organizing the fast; I couldn't very well not fast. So I did. In fact, we did a thirty-six-hour fast. We stopped eating after dinner on the Tuesday night before Ash

Wednesday, and we broke the fast on Thursday morning. Actually quite a long fast.

I did that for a number of years. Then I went off the Oxfam Board and the church was doing its own thing and I wasn't involved anymore, so I stopped fasting altogether. But in 1990 we started a committee to raise funds for Oxfam in New York City. And that's when we got the idea of doing fasts for sponsorship.

There were about one or two dozen fasters in the group and we each did it differently. I would send out letters to friends and business contacts, saying I was going to fast for twenty-four hours and asking them to pledge between $1 and $10 for every hour of the fast. I was writing to people in the financial community. Almost everybody could give me $24 and many could give at the top levels. But I did have one incredibly poor friend who could only give me $10. That was a stretch for her.

After about five years, the committee fell apart, but I kept fasting. I was doing my own thing—fasting and getting sponsors—and I have kept it up. I fast on the traditional Oxfam day—the Thursday before Thanksgiving, but every once in a while I will vary the day. I had my first visit to Paris on a fast day and there was no way I was going to fast on my first visit to Paris so I did the fast the day before. I once went downstairs to have my last meal in the company cafeteria before starting to fast and there wasn't a single appetizing thing to eat so I said, "Okay, fast started at lunch."

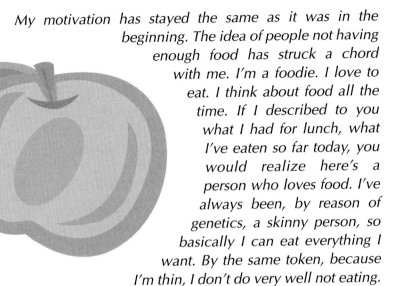

My motivation has stayed the same as it was in the beginning. The idea of people not having enough food has struck a chord with me. I'm a foodie. I love to eat. I think about food all the time. If I described to you what I had for lunch, what I've eaten so far today, you would realize here's a person who loves food. I've always been, by reason of genetics, a skinny person, so basically I can eat everything I want. By the same token, because I'm thin, I don't do very well not eating. (I do take fluids; I'm not trying to dehydrate myself.) My blood sugar plummets and I'm conscious of not being at my best, so I don't enjoy fasting. If I could achieve what I achieve for Oxfam without fasting, I wouldn't fast. It's something I do because I care about Oxfam.

My fasting gives the people who support me a connection to the agency and helps spread awareness of hunger in the world, and that's a good thing to do. I wish I could persuade some of them to fast and get their own sponsors, but I haven't turned the corner on that one yet. I think this year I may have my daughter persuaded. She's a high school teacher and she might get some of her students involved.

The Australian philosopher, Peter Singer, has articulated far better than I can some of the moral imperatives for supporting organizations like Oxfam. When you can do so, he says, with virtually no real sacrifice to yourself and at the same time make an incredible difference for others, a failure to do so is a serious moral failing. I find what he says congenial. I wish I had thought of saying it that way.

Stephen Land, a graduate of Harvard University (AB 1976, MBA/JD 1979), is a tax lawyer. He and his wife have two children and are members of the Larchmont Avenue Church in suburban Westchester County.

exploring a great spiritual practice

chaptereleven

PersonalFasting:
AsaDisciplineand
CompaniontoPrayer

Many people who see a deep spiritual connection between fasting and prayer do not participate in specific religious seasons like Lent or Ramadan. While there may be additional motives, fasting for them serves primarily as a way to enhance or intensify prayer. Often the prayer and the fasting seek answers to particular problems.

Most, but not all, of the Americans who speak of fasting in this connection are Christian. And most, but not all, are

Christians who describe themselves variously as evangelical Christians, Pentecostal Christians, or members of one of the free churches (those like the Quakers and the Baptists who have moved as far as possible from hierarchical models of church).

We will look first at the resurgence of fasting among evangelical Christians—at its vigor, its motivations, its challenges. We will next note some other traditions where fasting and prayer are closely woven, but unconnected to liturgical feasts or seasons.

Among Evangelicals: Fasting Reborn

In the last decade of the twentieth century, fasting among evangelical Christians in the United States experienced a strong resurgence. Following the leadership of popular preachers like Bill Bright, founder of Campus Crusade for Christ, and Jerry Falwell, chancellor of Liberty University and pastor of a Baptist mega-church in Virginia, hundreds of thousands, perhaps millions, of people have tried the discipline of fasting. For these men—and some of their followers—fasting has meant a forty-day biblical fast, during which they take only juice and water.

The resurgence is rooted in biblical models of fasting and in American Protestant history.

◆ As we have explored in earlier chapters, both the Hebrew and the Christian Scriptures offer many examples of prayer and fasting, sometimes for personal reasons, sometimes for the good of the community. Moses, Daniel, Esther, John the Baptist, Jesus, and then his disciples fasted as they prayed. Contemporary evangelical fasters often refer to biblical models, describing their fasts as, for example, a "Daniel fast," during which they may eat only fruits or nuts.

◆ Since the days of the early Puritan settlers, preachers have called for times of prayer and fasting, sometimes to bring their flocks back to a sense of personal discipline, sometimes to seek solutions—or forgiveness—for larger church or civic problems. The link between prayer and fasting was so solidly embedded in the country's religious heritage that in 1863 in the midst of the Civil War, Abraham Lincoln proclaimed a National Fast Day: "It behooves us then, to humble ourselves before the offended Power, to

"It behooves us then, to **humble** ourselves before the offended **Power**, to confess our national **sins**, and to **pray** for clemency and **forgiveness**."

National Fast Day

Abraham Lincoln

confess our national sins, and to pray for clemency and forgiveness."

This contemporary renewal of the discipline of fasting has reached a vast audience of many ages and backgrounds through the voices of individual preachers amplified by modern technologies.

One example makes the point. Bill Bright, who died in 2003, devoted the last years of his life to preaching the importance of fasting. He believed that God had called him to a forty-day fast, which he undertook in 1994. Transformed by its spiritual benefits and called by God to spread the word, as he wrote in his later books, he annually undertook similar fasts and also invited other evangelical church leaders to join him. Thousands of people have attended the yearly Prayer and Fasting conferences that Bright initiated, but millions more have accessed them through the Internet and at satellite sites in churches through the country. This successful outreach led Bright to say that by 1997, "two million courageous Christians . . . had responded to God's call to spend forty days in fasting and prayer for national and worldwide revival."

Motivations

For Bright and many other preachers in this tradition, fasting is clearly—and primarily—linked to what evangelical Christians call "the Great Commission"—the desire to bring new disciples to Christ. Fasting combined with prayer is "a spiritual atomic bomb," Bright says, that "releases the power of God" in individuals, in their church, and in their country.

But there are other significant reasons that evangelicals give for combining prayer and fasting.

Fasting combined with prayer is "a spiritual atomic bomb that releases the power of God."

Bill Bright

◆ Fasting is a way to get in touch with God. Whatever the other motivations, evangelicals say, fasting must be centered on God. Sometimes one experiences the presence of God directly. Sometimes the effects are more subtle, they warn, and we must settle for knowing only that we have honestly tried to make God, not food or some other craving, the focus of our lives.

◆ Fasting is a spiritual discipline. Richard J. Foster, whose book *Celebration of Discipline* has become a spiritual classic, says that fasting "reveals the things that control us. . . . We cover up what is inside us with food and other good things." Fasting moves us from concern about the shallow things of life into a deeper spiritual realm. There one can focus on what is really important and regain spiritual balance.

◆ It is important, evangelical Christians note, to view fasting not as drudgery but as a discipline filled with joy—one that releases the individual from self-centered preoccupations and compulsions and thus provides freedom. Foster writes: "Singing, dancing, even shouting characterize the disciplines of the spiritual life."

◆ Fasting is a way to seek answers for personal problems. Books on evangelical fasting are frequently filled with testimonials about the concrete results of fasting— restored health for a loved one, an end to infertility, a better job. Preachers warn their flocks that fasting must be God-centered and should not be used to manipulate God's will, but fasting for such personal answers remains popular.

Evangelical preachers note that fasting in times of great need, such as ill health, despair, or overwhelming sorrow, has deep biblical roots. It can be a special time for openness, a way to see God's presence in one's life and live out of that insight.

Challenges

■ ■ ■ ■ ■ ■ ■ ■ ■ ■ ■ ■ ■ ■ ■ ■

A long with this resurgence of interest in fasting among evangelical Christians has come a responsible critique. We note here three criticisms.

◆ Fasting is too goal-oriented. Twenty years ago, when *Celebration of Discipline* was first published, Foster wrote: "How easy it is to take something like fasting and try to use it to get God to do what we want. At times there is such stress upon the blessings and benefits of fasting that we would be tempted to believe that with a little fast we could have the world, including God, eating out of our hand."

A look at more recent evangelical literature shows that not much has changed. The goals may be either personal or focused on the wider community—from a local church's financial needs to the Great Awakening—but they remain items on the human agenda.

◆ A forty-day juice fast can be unhealthy for some people; fasting is too focused on food. Some evangelical Christians recommend shorter fasts. Jan Winebrenner, who writes for evangelical women, says that she often schedules a day or several days "of prayer and simple fare," during which she may eat only certain vegetables, fruits, salads, and soup. Such a routine, she says, does not interfere with an active lifestyle.

And, similar to the alternative Lenten fasting now occurring among Catholics and mainline Protestants, some evangelical Christians also say it is time to move away from America's obsession with food and fast from different, but equally addictive, behaviors.

◆ Contemporary evangelical fasting, by and large, does not connect the practice with concern for the poor and hungry of the world. While there are some popular outreach efforts, like World Vision's 30 Hour Famine (see chapter 10), most contemporary evangelical fasting remains focused on personal and national spiritual renewal.

Other Traditions

Among Christian religious traditions, we find that Mormons, in addition to their first-Sunday-of-the-month fasts (see chapter 4), also fast—either as individuals, as a family, or as a congregation—for particular reasons. They might fast to petition help for someone who is sick, for guidance in making a decision, before embarking on a difficult task, to overcome a particular weakness, or for comfort during a time of sorrow. Mormon literature offers some guidelines for such a fast: prayerful preparation, contemplation and meditation during the fast, a quiet cheerful attitude, and a prayer of thanksgiving when the fast ends.

Among eastern religions, Hindus also connect fasting with prayer. The Hindu calendar is filled with festivals that include fasting (see chapter 6). But, in addition, Hindus frequently fast on certain days of the week—every Tuesday, say—as a way of enhancing their prayer, finding internal peace, and seeking answers to specific requests.

Another group of people who value the important link between fasting and prayer are those who do not identify themselves with any particular religion. They may blend practices from both eastern and western traditions into their spiritual lives. And they may combine fasting with their practice of meditation or with an effort to align themselves to God's will. Fasting, they say, enhances their ability to sit quietly and listen to God instead of giving in to the pressures of modern life. Fasting enables them to focus solely on the present moment—not the tasks of the future and not the mistakes of the past.

For many people, those who have long known the power of fasting and those who have recently discovered fasting—from food or any other preoccupation—the discipline has become a steady and welcome companion to their prayer.

Voices

David Trembley

The first time I fasted it was a verbal fast. In the mid-70s, I was in business and thinking about serious spiritual things and I decided that I would be quiet for three days. I didn't do it for a historical or a reasoned theological position; I was just responding to my own spiritual needs. But the experience was so powerful. It slowed me down and let me pay attention to others. I had been so busy making my own noise that the other as other was never quite real to me.

Fasting from food has always been problematic for me. I dieted for years and years, but then I got over it. I have fasted from many other things. I'm an obsessive-compulsive personality. I get attached to activities that are not really the genuine article, they're substitutes for it. For example, one of the things I really loved was the mail. Partly I guess that came from being a freelance writer for thirty years and waiting for the check to come. So I designed a week when I didn't touch the mail. I was hoping to make myself more aware of what really matters and less consumed with what doesn't. Does that make sense?

For me, and I think this is true for many of us, the first thing you have to do is strip away. That's the fasting part. As soon as I find something in my life that is distracting my attention in a consistent way from the things that really matter, then I have to move that thing as gently as possible out of my way. I used to call that fasting. But now that term seems so clunky and mechanical. I think now I move into the stripping away in a more graceful, more natural way because it's the way God works with my spirit.

Why I got rid of the term "fast" is that so many people think it's negative. I tell people that what we're here for is joy. Find the joy—notice I don't say happiness—in the fasting. Yes, there's a bit of a loss in there, because you are taking something out of your life, something you were using to blind you to deeper things. But there's something in the actual process of letting go, which is holy. It's not just that I'm doing it in order to get something, but there's something in the very process that's holy.

The reasons we do things are as important as the activities. I think you could probably do fasting for personal spiritual benefit, because life is better. But for me there is that Divine otherness, which is what it's really all about. What is prayer but anything and everything we do on purpose to get in touch and stay in touch with God? That has been so freeing for me and it fits with my fasting. I mean it's right there—hand and glove.

I'm now old enough to have thought of my own mortality, to take it seriously, and not pretend that I'm never going to die. And the more I think that way, the more I realize how incredibly narrow our perspectives are. Prayer and fasting invite me to see that God is everywhere all the time and to begin to pay attention.

David Trembley, 61, is an American Baptist minister. He and his wife, Lo-Ann, are co-pastors of an inner-city congregation in Milwaukee, Wisconsin. They are the authors of several spiritual books, the latest of which is *The Gratitude Attitude.*

Voices

Sudha Dubey Newman

[Fasting] has many meanings to me, actually, not just one meaning. When I was very young [growing up in India in a Hindu family], it was a family tradition: Everyone fasted on certain days or certain festivals. So it came to me very easily. When my mother was fasting or my father was fasting, the whole family was fasting. You fasted without even thinking about it much. And it had a religious meaning for them, but to me at the time it was just something other people were doing, so I had to do it, too.

You know, Hinduism is a very, very liberal religion. Nobody tells you what to do or not to do. And you follow or you don't follow. But as I was growing older, fasting became, at a certain point, very religious to me. I prayed every day and then I fasted for certain days. And the days I was fasting I was more calm.

It wasn't total fasting [like in other religions]. It was restraining yourself from a lot of heavy foods, but there were some things like tapioca or fruits or nuts that you could eat. It was more like cleansing yourself. For years I fasted once a week. I did Tuesdays. And then for years I fasted every Monday. Weekends were always heavy eating and I began to see a nutritional incentive to add to my religious reasons. On Mondays I would not eat for half a day. After that, I would eat a little something. At the end of each fast day, at five o'clock, six o'clock, I would eat a vegetarian dinner.

I could fast then much more than I can now, but I still occasionally fast ten Mondays, ten Tuesdays, or ten somethings. When I'm worried about something, maybe somebody's health, if I fast, I feel I'm doing something to face the situation. People always say, "Well, what are we going to do about this or that?" Fasting is a way for me to relieve the tension. I think fasting gives you time to sort out problems, to meditate about solutions.

I pray every day in the morning or before I eat my main dinner and it's a very short prayer. When I'm fasting, I may say to God that this is my situation, this is how I'm handling it, and please help me. For five minutes, ten minutes, I concentrate within myself, and think of why I'm fasting. It's not like penance. It's just bringing myself together.

Fasting also helped me to understand how it hurts to be hungry. And I tell you the truth: my mother died of cancer of the esophagus; she could not have an operation. She was eating only some biscuits and a little water. Each time I fast, I *always think of her and how she suffered being hungry all the time. I don't think you think about these things when you're young, but, at my age, I meditate on all those things and I feel for other people. It's helped me to understand myself, my family, and the people who are suffering.*

I understand all these reasons—that for me fasting is religious, it's personal, it's psychological, it's all kinds of things. I don't really have to analyze it. Luckily I've married a husband who is absolutely wonderful and always I have full freedom. He's a sweet man, and he follows his practices, and I follow mine.

Now I haven't fasted for, I don't know, six months. I pray every day, but I feel like I'm not complete. I want to start fasting again, but you have to know yourself. When I'm ready, I'll do it. Right now I don't have to fast. If some crisis or some problem comes and I feel really disturbed, if I have tension over something, I'll fast.

Sudha Dubey Newman, 62, was born and brought up in a Brahmin family in northern India. She was educated in India and Australia, where she lived for sixteen years with her Jewish American husband. They now live in Marblehead, Massachusetts, where Sudha works at the public library.

exploring a great spiritual practice

chaptertwelve

HolisticFasting: TheBodyMind SpiritConnection

All of the fasting disciplines we have thus far discussed, be they religious or secular, personal or political, are actually examples of holistic fasting. It is an important point because the term "holistic" describes the essential connection of mind, body, and spirit that exists in each of us, no matter how we understand our own "soul" or express our spirituality. And holistic fasting honors that connection.

When we listen to the voices of people who describe their experiences of fasting, we hear two levels of reality. They speak of their physical reactions—hunger, headaches, fatigue or, alternatively, improved energy and clarity of mind— and their spiritual responses—peace, inner discipline, a deeper awareness of themselves, a connection with something beyond themselves, which they may describe as God or the hungry people of the world. Whatever language they use or whatever motivated their fast, they are expressing a relationship between the physical and the spiritual.

Once we acknowledge the essential link between the physical and the spiritual, it becomes a question of emphasis. Some fasting, such as that for a Yom Kippur, has an obviously spiritual focus. In this chapter, we focus on fasting that specifically highlights an individual's mind-body-spirit connection. Here fasting is meant to achieve a kind of self-healing, to cleanse, detoxify, or balance the body so that the spirit is free to follow enriching pursuits.

Contemporary spirituality is filled with choices; many different roads can lead to the same goal. We will take a closer look at three holistic paths. Each path can offer wisdom, but each, taken to some popular extremes, contains risky physical practices.

Fasting is meant to achieve a kind of self-healing, to cleanse, detoxify, or balance the body so that the spirit is free to follow enriching pursuits.

◆ From India come *Ayurveda*, a natural healing system, and yoga, a discipline that has been described as "being centered in action."

◆ From China come the Taoist traditions of *Qigong* (pronounced "chee gong"), a system that releases and transfers energy, and *bigu*, a fast that benefits from energy transfer.

◆ From contemporary American society come insights from health food advocates and restorative spas.

From India

*A*yurveda, which translates as "the science of life," has its roots in ancient India. In the 1980s it became widespread in the Western world through the work of Maharishi Mahesh Yogi and Deepak Chopra, whom *Time Magazine* has called, "the poet-prophet of alternative medicine." Chopra believes that the ancient practices of holistic medicine provide self-healing techniques that western medicine, with its emphasis on drug therapy and high technology, has overlooked.

The goal of *Ayurveda* is integration of body, mind, and spirit. To keep the body healthy and the mind calm, *Ayurveda* employs a variety of natural methods: herbal medicines, yoga, meditation, massage, and cleansing.

A deep cleansing fast is central to the process. Practitioners say one cannot achieve total well being, balancing body, mind, and spirit, if the body is filled with toxins. A cleansing fast in the *ayurvedic* tradition usually prescribes a very limited diet, which may be simply a vegan regimen, in which the participants eat only certain fruits and vegetables, or it may be limited to *kitchari* (an Indian soup made with rice, mung beans and spices) and herbal teas. Whatever foods are allowed, the cleansing fast is designed to give the digestive system a rest and clean out the kidneys, liver, and intestines. Colon cleansing may also be part of the treatment.

Ayurvedic fasting, which may last as long as seven or nine days and is frequently done "on location" at a yoga studio or wellness center, is usually accompanied by herbal therapy, massage, yoga, and meditation. The herbs are prescribed to revitalize one's depleted system; oil massages are meant to aid in detoxification; yoga postures strengthen and soothe the body but can also deepen a meditation practice. The fast itself may improve meditation because energy diverted from digestion can be directed to peaceful contemplation.

It is the meditation that links the physical cleansing to the spiritual dimension. Participants say that daily yoga practice and meditation allow them to experience the benefits of fasting in a calmer, less reactive way. They find it easier to reach their inner selves and they are at peace with what they find there. That spiritual dimension is what they would like to retain—to transform their otherwise hectic, stress-filled lives.

What are the challenges of *ayurvedic* fasting? As is common in any long-term fasting regimen—anything longer than twenty-four hours—people experience headaches, diarrhea, constipation, and fatigue. Proponents say that these symptoms usually disappear by the third or fourth day, that the accompanying therapies will forestall any serious health crises, and that the end results—a detoxified body, improved digestion and elimination, and an overall sense of well-being and rejuvenation—are worth the struggle.

Some yoga masters disagree. They may prefer shorter fasts—one day a week drinking only water, juice, or both—as a way to reach the same goal, or they are unconvinced by any advantages of *ayurvedic* fasting. One yogini (a serious, female practitioner of yoga) who has been studying and teaching Iyengar yoga for more than for thirty years sees spiritual as well as physical danger: "Fasting loosens your hold on yourself. You can lose your I." She believes that yoga practice, like Buddhism, is built on moderation. There is no spiritual or physical need, she says, to deplete the body of food or sleep if one is truly living the discipline of a yoga life.

From China

ike Ayurveda from India, the Chinese natural self-healing system is thousands of years old. The tradition is based on an understanding of qi (also spelled chi, and pronounced "chee") as the vital energy that courses through our bodies. Channels of qi flow along paths that link the internal organs with external ones; illness can result when qi is blocked or imbalanced, accumulating in one area of the body and depriving another area of its vital energy. In Taoist thought qi is what stitches body and spirit together. Qi is also universal energy, present in the world around us—in other people, in nature, the atmosphere. And that energy, too, can be released, transferred, and absorbed.

Qigong, then, is a set of exercises that releases and transfers the flow of energy from one part of the body to another and also from the universe to a particular person, and that concept underlies the Taoist cleansing fast known as bigu (pronounced "be goo").

As in Ayurveda, the goal of bigu is to detoxify the body naturally to restore or maintain good health and inner peace.

The regimen is also similar. Practitioners, working under the guidance of a master or instructor, eat a very limited amount of certain fruits and vegetables for a period of at least three days and frequently for seven days or more, even going as long as three months. The key to surviving—and benefiting from—such a long arduous fast, advocates say, is the energy the fasters receive from their environment. An inexhaustible supply of energy can be transferred from nature to the body as nourishment. If the transfer of energy is effective enough, the faster experiences no suffering. As one *bigu* faster described her experience in an issue of *Qi Journal,* "Who would have thought I would come to believe that I could eat the Sun and the Moon? Now I do."

This transfer of energy comes through *Qigong,* sometimes mediated by a master and sometimes accessed by an individual's own meditation. Once again, we see similarities with the Indian tradition. In the Taoist tradition, meditation is also the link to the spiritual dimension of fasting. Beginning with guided-imagery meditation, which may be focused simply on moving *qi* through the body, and progressing to empty-mind meditation, a practitioner moves from a focus on her own energy to an awareness of her personal spirit (*shen*) and ultimately to participation in universal consciousness (*tao*). Thus, advocates say, a person practicing *Qigong* can ultimately arrive at a sense of spiritual connectedness to everybody and everything in the universe.

What are the cautions to *bigu*? *Bigu* proponents say that the transfer of *qi* forestalls any serious problems. Still, they will agree, it should never be attempted without the guidance of a master, someone who has practiced *Qigong* extensively and is no further than a phone call away. Because *bigu* is most often undertaken by people who have some symptoms of ill health and who are hoping for a cure, individual attention is essential. If the meditations aren't working, the transfer of energy isn't happening and the practitioner is suffering, the master will recommend the fast be ended. As we saw with fasting in the *Ayurvedic* tradition, so with *bigu*: many within the Chinese medical tradition do not accept the necessity of such a fast.

From the West

The topic of fasting has long been part of alternative medicine. Paul and Patricia Bragg's book, *The Miracle of Fasting* and Stanley Burroughs' *The Master Cleanser* have been on the shelves of health food stores for decades. An array of newer entries provides variations on the basic message: a fast, often in this context called a diet, is good for the body. Because it eliminates toxins and gives digestive tract organs a rest, fasting purifies the body, preserves energy, and helps one get more out of a longer, healthier life. In recent years, fasting has moved from a practice that appealed to a small group of the already-sick to a much larger audience of people who are reasonably healthy and want to remain so.

In the health food literature there are many kinds of fasts: water fasts, juice fasts, oatmeal fasts, fruit and vegetable fasts, to name only a few. One can undertake a fast alone—guided by a book, a local storeowner, an online website—or at a spa in the company of other fasters and have access to activities such as massage, nutrition, and exercise classes.

We will look more closely at both options, assessing the spiritual dimensions and noting risks.

Fasting at home has some obvious advantages. It can be done while honoring daily commitments like job and family. It is far cheaper than going to a spa for a weeklong "vacation." Juice fasts have traditionally been the most popular at-home fasts. According to proponents, they are also the safest. Buy a blender; drink your meals as fruit and vegetable juices or soups and add herbal teas, if you wish. You can view this fast as a liquid vegan diet, one that rests the organs while providing alkaline-based nutrition. To achieve the desired cleansing, four days is the suggested minimum fast.

Another popular and far more extreme fast is called either the "Master Cleanse," from its roots in the Burroughs book, or "the lemonade fast." Here the faster consumes only water and lemon juice with a bit of cayenne pepper and a small amount of honey or maple syrup. While some proponents speak of the energy and improved moods they experienced, many others who have tried the lemonade fast talk of the negative effects. "I was a mess," says one man. "I had no energy. I was miserable during—and afterward."

The spiritual dimension of this kind of fasting is unclear. Some fasters make time for daily meditation and find in their renewed energy a stronger commitment to a deeper, finer life. Others are satisfied to concentrate solely on physical results and expect only weight loss or improved digestion and elimination.

Anyone who tries an at-home fast, especially a lemonade fast, for a long period of time—anything more than a day or two—needs to be in close touch with an experienced professional and should also speak to a doctor before beginning such a regimen. There is no way to predict how any individual's body will react to such an extended challenge. One can do harm, finding anxiety, tension, and ill health instead of peace.

Spa fasting also offers some benefits and some drawbacks. Participants are away from home and away from daily routines and daily temptations. They are in the company of knowledgeable people (assuming they've chosen the spa carefully) and others who are fasting. The diet is carefully planned and will usually include herbal supplements; days and nights are filled with activities that distract from hunger pangs. And fasters can access a spiritual dimension, as they choose, in the natural surroundings, in yoga, meditation, prayer, or simply solitude.

On the other hand, spa fasting is expensive—a one-week session can run upward from $2000—and may require a long trip to a remote desert or mountain location. While the spiritual benefits may hold in the protected spa environment, they can be hard to maintain back in the real world.

A Final Word

In concluding this chapter, I'll give a voice to many western doctors, nurses, and nutritionists who urge caution for anyone undertaking a long holistic fast, whether it is based on eastern self-healing systems or in the literature of alternative medicine. Many of these professionals say that such fasting is unnecessary for good health; a body that is routinely disciplined in its choices of food and exercise is far preferable. The ideal is moderation, and the risks of such fasting are real. Others in the field stress that there is nothing "dirty" about our bodies that makes them in need of "cleansing."

Self-healing is a worthwhile goal; at the very least, it places responsibility for maintaining good health on each individual. But holistic fasting, like all other kinds of fasting, requires a responsible understanding of motives and methods.

Andy Rosenfarb

I've been studying medical Qigong for more than ten years. I began my studies in Chinese medicine after attending college. Then I earned my Masters at Pacific College of Oriental Medicine in San Diego and continued post-graduate studies at a Zhejiang College and University hospital in China. I currently apprentice with a Qigong master here in the United States, Master Bin Hui He.

I'm not perfect with my diet throughout the year—I occasionally eat on the run like most people—and I accumulate food toxins. So I use an ancient system called bigu *or high-energy fasting to detox—in order to get the hormonal toxins out, to get the antibiotics out, to remove all the junk that's accumulated in my body from the food I've been eating.*

At first, I found fasting rather challenging. I did a nine-day bigu my first time. It was very uncomfortable for the first three days or so. Master He told me that this is a normal reaction and part of the process. He's a Chinese medical doctor and has guided more than 10,000 people through the bigu process. After the first three days, Master He said, "Andy, you're very healthy, and your system is now detoxing. I think you can hang in there for nine days." He said, "Just take it day by day." And so I did—while silently cursing him for making me do this for nine days. It wasn't until completing bigu that I understood that I just had to get over "the hump" and the suffering would diminish. For someone who hasn't had any experience with any type of fasting, detoxification can be a grim process that is seemingly endless.

Toward the end of my nine-day fast, I had one of the most pronounced experiences of mental, emotional, and spiritual clarity. The whole world seemed to be operating in slow motion. It was just awesome! From the time I was a little kid, I was used to this fast-paced life style. The fasting just slowed everything down for me. Everything seemed to be so crystal clear. Everything had such vibrant colors and sounds. All my sensory perceptions were incredibly heightened. Life just had a lot more life in it. I became very sensitive not only to myself, but to patients I had been treating while on bigu. I also picked up on things in my environment that I hadn't had time to see before.

That first time I did bigu, I did a half-day of Qigong meditation, and the other half, I saw patients in my clinic. But

I feel lucky that I found a Qigong *master who is very nearby geographically. During the first* bigu *process it is very important to be under close supervision. The first couple of days, especially for a beginner, it is important to spend much time meditating in order to increase the body's energy supply. After doing* bigu *a few times, the ability to cultivate energy through* Qigong *meditation becomes second nature. With good* Qigong *practice, you can go to work and can do just about whatever you want. You fast for as long as you feel well.*

I was able to persuade both my father and my grandfather to try bigu. *Generally speaking, beginners who have more weight have an easier time with* bigu. *than thin people. My father is somewhat overweight and he did not experience any intense hunger pains. In fact, he felt great. I'm thin and I had a much more difficult time with my blood sugar and with hunger pains. For my grandfather,* bigu *fasting was very much a psycho-spiritual and emotional healing process. Being a survivor from a concentration camp in World War II, his relationship to food is very different from most people. In his mind, food is more valuable than gold.*

I explained to my grandfather, "Gramps, you've got to not eat for a couple of days and you also have to meditate." He didn't believe he could do it at all. For him it was so scary. But my grandfather is a very positive and happy guy—which is not common for a survivor of a World War II concentration camp. It was amazing to watch him go through the fast and see how empowered he became. He shocked himself that he could go without eating—and feel good. He had never meditated before, but he did it and he was positive about it.

My grandfather had been experiencing benign tumors that had continued to grow on his bladder for years. Every year, his physician would remove the tumors, and every year they would grow back. It's been nearly three years since he did bigu and the tumors have not returned. He has done nothing else that could be attributed to his healing.

These days, I do a few mini-fasts and one major fast a year. That's become routine for me, something I do every year. Occasionally, I will teach people who are interested how to do bigu. It's empowering to know that there are techniques like bigu that help me have a positive influence over my own health and longevity. What it comes down to is this: continuing to learn and teach as many people as I can how to live healthfully.

Andy Rosenfarb, 31, is National Board Certified in Acupuncture and Chinese Herbal medicine. He also practices and teaches Tai Chi and medical *Qigong*. He is currently in private practice in New Jersey.

exploring a great spiritual practice

FinalThoughts

n the beginning of our search, we confronted the basic question: why fast? In the intervening chapters, we explored ancient and contemporary motives and methods: why people fast and how they fast. As we pull together the threads we have followed and attempt to weave a conclusion, we have a few remaining tasks.

Distilling the Wisdom

◆ Fasting, as we have discovered, has been a universal practice. There are a variety of seasons and reasons for fasting. But, unless one follows the observances of Yom Kippur, Roman Catholic or Eastern Orthodox Lent, or Ramadan, there are no rules. The challenge for each of us is to determine where we fit. If we decide to fast, how and when and why will we fast?

◆ Fasting is not the only—or even the primary—spiritual discipline. In Christianity and Judaism, fasting, joined with prayer and almsgiving, is part of a threefold spiritual message. In Islam, it is one of Five Pillars of holiness. We are challenged to keep fasting in perspective. While we cannot place it front and center, can we continue to ignore it?

◆ Healthy spirituality honors body and soul. And a spiritually healthy attitude toward fasting also acknowledges the integrity of the human person. We are reminded of the words of Rabbi Bonder: "God resides in a person who is a whole being." Maintaining that balance—that wholeness—is our challenge.

◆ By exploring the practice of fasting across many traditions, we have attempted to augment our own perhaps sketchy knowledge of fasting. Catholics who thought of fasting only as tired prohibitions against eating meat might be energized by insights from those who fast for peace and justice. Those who have rejected all liturgical seasons might be touched by the eastern tradition of *ahimsa* or the role fasting plays in deepening meditation. Now is the time to assess: how has our understanding of the practice of fasting been enriched?

> "God resides in a person who is a whole being."
> *Rabbi Bonder*

Making Careful Choices

We have focused on a core of wisdom but also noted, in every chapter, a variety of extreme customs. Dangerous fasting practices are deep-rooted in history but also quite clearly present in contemporary society. Sister Joan Chittister's words echo: "It is so easy to ply extremes and miss the river of tradition."

◆ Spiritual writers place the practice of fasting under the umbrella of the virtue of temperance. In all traditions, moderation is the key. Contemporary spirituality does not indulge in self-centered and punishing asceticism, slide into yo-yo dieting, or trigger a serious eating disorder.

◆ The difficulty of fasting—from food or any other compulsion—in a consumer-driven culture where instant gratification has become the norm is apparent. Fasting is counter-cultural; those who would fast will have to be highly motivated. They would do well to seek guidance and support—from prayer, from others, from spiritual reading. Recall the Buddhist principle of "right association": by associating with and imitating those whose spirit we see as holy, we can make progress along the Way.

Listening to the Spirit

Whether we speak of following an Inner Voice or of listening, like Elijah on the mountain, for God's quiet murmur, the decision to fast is a very personal one. For each of us, the discipline could look different. It could accept or decline certain foods and liquids; it could last a shorter or longer period of time; it could be a one-time or a regular experience.

My task has been to present a full range of information. In the end, each of us will choose whether or not to follow an inner prompt. It is worth repeating here the words of Rabbi Heschel: "The higher goal of spiritual living is not to amass a wealth of information, but to face sacred moments."

"The **higher** goal of **spiritual** living is not to amass a wealth of information, but to face **sacred** moments."

Rabbi Heschel

A Standard of Measure

In 1967, a year before he was assassinated, the Reverend Dr. Martin Luther King, Jr. gave a sermon he called "The Three Dimensions of a Complete Life."

Dr. King suggested that we view our spiritual lives as three-dimensional. The first dimension, which he calls length, is "the dimension of life where we are concerned with developing our inner powers." King says, "There is such a thing as rational and healthy self-interest," but focus only on our inner life is not a complete life. "A lot of people never get beyond the first dimension of life." It is necessary, he says, to add a second dimension, breadth, to length. "The breadth of life is the outward concern for the welfare of others. . . . a man has not begun to live until he can rise above the narrow confines of his own individual concerns to the broader concerns of all humanity." The third dimension, height, is our upward reach toward God. If life is to be complete, King says, "we must move beyond our self-interest. We must move beyond humanity and reach up, way up for the God of the universe."

We can tap into Dr. King's three-dimensional imagery and use it as a standard of measure to evaluate the practice of fasting in contemporary spirituality.

◆ Does fasting enhance the "length" of our lives? Does it move us toward an integration of body and soul?

As we have seen, fasting is a holistic practice; it has both physical and spiritual ramifications. Fasting, whether one chooses a traditional abstinence from food or an alternative constraint, is a spiritual discipline that allows us to assert control over our impulses, to move deeper into our best selves. It may be difficult; we may fail.

Certainly we will become more aware of our human limitations. True spiritual fasting views the body as holy and aims for personal freedom, growth, and inner peace.

◆ Does fasting affect the "breadth" of our lives? Does it acknowledge concern for the lives and needs of others?

This outward focus of fasting surfaces again and again in the wisdom of many religious traditions. The prophet Isaiah, one of the earliest voices we heard, said that proper fasting is not "a day for men to starve their bodies" but a time to display both charity ("share your bread with the hungry") and social justice ("let the oppressed go free"). His words should reach not only Jews and Christians but all spiritual seekers. Proper fasting should somehow connect each of us with the poor, the hungry, and the oppressed.

Contemporary discussion also recognizes the needs of the planet. Fasting can help us confront our society's rampant consumption of the earth's limited resources. It can also put us in touch with the rhythms of natural world. We can come to a deeper appreciation of the ancient cycles of planting seeds and gathering the harvest, then waiting again, in hunger, for new life.

◆ Does our fasting reach out to the third spiritual dimension and enhance our awareness of God?

Whatever we call the presence of the Divine in our lives—God, Yahweh, Allah, Spirit, Brahman, Universal

Consciousness—we can ask: is our fasting an encounter with the sacred? Does it put us in touch with the Divine? When we fast, we meet up with our human limits. When we fast, we dare to confront those limitations and open ourselves to ultimate mystery. If we take advantage of the encounter and pray, we express our awareness not only of our own human limitation but also of the presence of God. We follow the example of wisdom figures from many traditions who have found that prayer and fasting are inextricably linked.

Our answers to these questions will, I think, tell us if the practice of fasting is a wise path leading toward our ultimate goal. If the discipline serves as an expression of our love— proper love of ourselves, love for others, and love for God— we can say it is a worthwhile spiritual endeavor, still relevant in the twenty-first century.

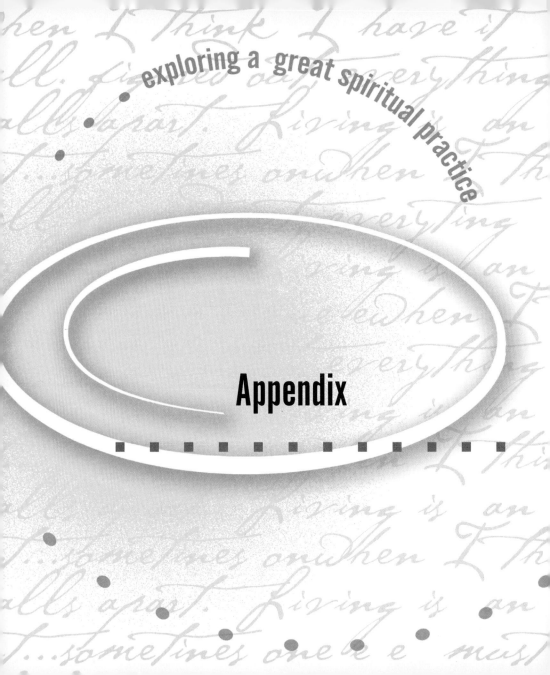

exploring a great spiritual practice

Appendix

The Physical Challenges

Fasting, unlike most other spiritual disciplines, has an obvious physical factor. It is imperative to take seriously the body's health during a fast. Throughout the book, although we focused on the spiritual dimension, the words of wisdom figures and the voices of ordinary people offered some practical suggestions on the physical aspects of fasting.

For those who may still have questions, here is additional advice gathered from medical professionals, spiritual directors, and those who have fasted.

◆ If you have any doubt about your body's ability to go without food or liquid for a period of time, consult your doctor first. No religious traditions require fasting if someone has medical conditions that will cause ill health. And, certainly, no personal fasting should take that risk.

◆ Doctors and nutritionists say that a short fast—twenty-four or thirty-six hours without food—will probably not cause any harm for most healthy people. No beginner, medical professionals say, should undertake a long fast without qualified supervision. Long fasts deplete the body's nutritional reserves and can have a variety of serious consequences. It takes time and experience to understand how your body will respond to the challenge of fasting.

◆ If you decide to try fasting, start slowly. You could give up one meal occasionally to see how your body tolerates the absence of food before you lengthen the fast to two meals, which is a twenty-four-hour fast, or three meals, which can be a thirty-six-hour fast, depending on when you start. Do not be tempted to eat an extra heavy meal just before you fast. Eat normally.

◆ Unless a religious tradition forbids it, drink plenty of water and do not allow yourself to become dehydrated. Do not, in any case, go more than twenty-four hours without water. On some fasts you may take fruit and vegetable juices—and perhaps clear soups and herbal teas—in addition to water.

◆ In most cases, people do not drink alcohol, soda, or coffee while they are fasting. You may have caffeine withdrawal symptoms, usually headaches, if you are a moderate to heavy coffee drinker. Some experienced fasters try to relinquish the caffeine well before the start of a fast so they eliminate the double challenge of hunger and caffeine withdrawal.

◆ When you come to the end of the fast, do not immediately go back to your normal diet. Eat lightly at first. Avoid heavy foods. The longer you have fasted, the longer "re-entry" time you will need.

◆ Fasting is not a substitute for dieting. You will probably not lose weight on a proper fast. You may lose a few pounds temporarily, but the weight usually returns when you resume normal eating patterns.

◆ While fasting, people experience a variety of physical reactions. You will no doubt be hungry. You may be tired or listless or have trouble concentrating. You may have headaches; you may experience other uncomfortable signs that your body is adjusting to an empty stomach. The medical professionals say that if at any time during a fast you experience any seriously distressing symptoms, stop the fast. Return to eating—slowly.

CAROLE GARIBALDI ROGERS is a professional writer, editor and oral historian. She has written numerous magazine and newspaper articles for publications such as *America* and *The New York Times.* This is her sixth book. Ms. Rogers received an MA in theology from the College of Saint Elizabeth where she currently directs an oral history project. She lives in Morristown, New Jersey, with her husband, Leo. They are the parents of two grown sons.